Prayers by a Prisoner

For Peace, Healing, and Hope

Aubrey Lee Price

Copyright 2017 by Aubrey Lee Price

Request for information should be addressed to
Twil Publishing, LLC
PO Box 10144
Bradenton, Fl. 34282

ISBN No. 978-1542734738
ISBN: 1542734738

Scripture taken from the New American Standard Bible, Copyright 1960, 1962, 1963, 1968, 1971, 1972, 1973, 1975, 1977, 1995 by the Lockman Foundation. Used by permission. www.Lockman.org

All rights reserved. No part of this publication may be reproduced, stored in a retrieval system, or transmitted in any form or by any means—electronic, mechanical, photocopy, recording, or any other—except for brief quotations in printed reviews, without the prior permission of the publisher.

Printed in the United States of America.

This book is dedicated to

My mom and dad

They showed me the Father's love.

Contents

Acknowledgments
Introduction
  1. Wasted Time
  2. Waiting Time
  3. A New Day
  4. A Starting Point for Change
  5. Peace with God
  6. A Clean Heart
  7. Forgiveness
  8. The Poison That Kills
  9. Forbidden Desires
10. Pouring Out
11. Confinement to Conformity
12. Cries of Depression
13. Seasoned by Fire
14. Passion for God
15. Hope Is Not My Enemy
16. "Chuck Norris"
Bibliography
Appendix 1 – Thirty Must-Read Books for the Growing Christian
Appendix 2 – A Short History of the Bible
Notes

Introduction

I want to explain that I am a fellow struggler in Christ. I am not infallible, and thankfully, I have abandoned the God complex. My flaws and mistakes are obvious, and I say along with the apostle Paul that I am the chief of all sinners. This book is not about any extraordinary knowledge or insight that I have attained. It is simply about the practices and habits that God has led me to develop to make the most of my time in prison and the remainder of my life. I am a learner, an avid reader, and a lifelong student of contemplative prayer. I am always asking God to make the necessary changes that He knows I need to implement in order for me to conform to the image of Christ.

Just because I am a Christian does not mean I am without troubles, pain, and suffering. We, who have served time or are serving time in prison, know the affliction and darkness we experience in prison. We have been through the inhumane, harsh, and brutal process of eternal condemnation. We are alienated, isolated, and despised by society. Our names have become a reproach. The odds of any kind of comeback are stacked against us. The world looks upon us as pariah and with contempt. Many of us are rejected and forsaken and wrestle with feelings of deep loneliness, abandonment, and overwhelming regret. We wonder if there is any hope.

The good news for us is that Jesus repeatedly gave dignity back to the despised. Others may look at us with scorn, but Jesus makes us human again. Here is the bottom line: God knows everything about us—every hidden sin. He knows every thought we've had, every step that we've taken, and every word we've spoken. He knows the intentions of our hearts. He knows all the things we've seen and done that make us want to run, hide, and even die. And yet He loves us.

Jesus is a friend and lover of sinners like you and me, and there is nothing we can do to make Him stop loving us. He meets us where we are. He disciplines and corrects us when necessary. He forgives our past. He overwhelms us with His love, and He gives us an eternal home in Heaven. Nothing can separate us from His infinite love. Because of this, we can say along with the psalmist, "I will not die, but live, and tell of the works of the Lord. The Lord has disciplined me severely, but He has not given me over to death" (Ps. 118:17–19).

    This book is about calling out to our loving and compassionate God in desperation, brokenness, and humility. It is about believing in Him to bring peace, healing, and hope to our lives. It is about making the most of the second chances He gives us. It is about having confidence in our prayers and finding the beauty of God in the darkness we face.

    There is nothing more encouraging than the fact that any person, though his or her sins and poor choices have placed him or her in the belly of despair, still has the opportunity and ability to connect with the source of all life. As a result, the person is consciously able to change from something dreary to something of beauty and hope. I am confident that what you read in this book will turn all the odds in your favor. The habit of our thinking and actions will change as God honors and answers our prayers. He hears our desperate cries. He will not turn away from the cries of His children. He will turn our despair into hope, our darkness into light, and bring us back from death and into newness of life.

Chapter 1: Wasted Time

Wait for the Lord, be strong and take heart, and wait for the Lord.
—Psalms 27:14

The prison as a waiting place is a hard place. Most people in the free world think of waiting in terms of traffic jams, restaurant lines, and the doctor's office. In the Bible, Abraham and Sarah waited for eighty years for the promised son of Isaac. Joseph was sold into slavery and betrayed by his own murderous brothers at the age of seventeen. He then spent thirteen years in an Egyptian prison waiting on God's deliverance. Moses, who committed murder and fled as fugitive from Egypt, had to wait forty years on the backside of the desert in Midian in quiet preparation and training before God finally called him to lead the Israelites to salvation from their oppression. David ran for thirteen years as a fugitive from King Saul living in various caves waiting for the kingship of Israel. Israel waited for twenty-five hundred years for the promised Messiah. The church has now waited two thousand years for Christ's return.

Some experience the pain of waiting for a loved one to return from a faraway place or from a place of suffering like prison. A few think about waiting in terms of the one they love, like the Old Testament patriarch Jacob. He loved Rachel and patiently waited for her for seven years. Then he had to work another seven years just so he could keep her because he was deceived by her father, Laban, on his wages. For Jacob, the seven years went by like a few days to him because he loved her so much.[1] Most believe that true love is worth the wait. Time went by fast because of blissful love.

One of my past cellmates was usually very talkative. One day I noticed him working hard on a very lengthy twenty-page letter. During that day he did not take time to talk to another person, including me, for even a small break in time. He was so focused in his devotion to the letter that he spent the entire day writing his most intimate thoughts down. He skipped breakfast, lunch, and dinner and wrote even after lights-out. Why? Because he was writing to the one he loved—a girlfriend who had forgotten him and was now with someone else. Love, separation, and jealousy change everything.

We prisoners know that conquering the impatience of waiting for months and years is no easy task. It can become everything. One year is 365 days. Three years is 1,095 days. Before I began my incarceration period, I completed 1,052 sleepless nights of extreme depression and anxiety. Finding rest and peace was no small dilemma. The year 2011 was the time when the wrath of God came upon my life. I could not make even one good decision. Nothing disturbs the mind like being consistently wrong. It was not until May of 2014 that I finally stopped fighting God. From April of 2011 until May of 2014, four and a half months after first being incarcerated, I finally trusted God again and slept through the night. God sent me some help from my "prison tested" cellmate and one-armed friend named Lucky. I had to relearn how to be still, cease striving, and know that He is God.[2] During those days of depression, and then another 1,095 days in prison, there had been times that minutes went by like hours. Hours went by like days. And days, like months.

Some of that time was spent in the very restricted environment of solitary confinement where the stress and irritation became my only focus. So far, I have spent a little over five months in solitary confinement. It is a horrible place of torture and abuse. I can't count the times when I thought the waiting would never end. Hope of my release from solitary was always met with some kind of bureaucratic prison delay. Proverbs 13 tells us that hope deferred makes the heart sick, and hope had often become my enemy during many painful struggles of the past six years. The seemingly endless periods of waiting can lead to insanity. I have seen firsthand the permanent effects of mental and psychological damage to other inmates.

In those four walls of claustrophobic darkness, I prayed like I needed air to breath and oxygen to fill my blood. I prayed and prayed and prayed. I drew close to God. I set my heart only on Him. Prayer sustained me.

Nelson Mandela spent an unbelievable twenty-seven unjust and harsh years waiting for his release from prison, and as he testifies, it was only by God's grace that he came out with a spirit of love and reconciliation instead of revenge and retaliation.

Baloney Man

To my amazement I have met many others who have done years in solitary confinement. As a young man who lived in the projects of

South Atlanta, my friend, nicknamed Rooster, had stabbed an officer in the face in a fit of foolish rage. While he did not kill the officer, it took him many years of prison and solitary confinement before he would acknowledge the evil and wickedness of his actions. He told me the story of how he spent seven years in solitary, eating lots of baloney, staring at four walls and trying to maintain his sanity.

Forsaken by his distant family, forgotten by old friends and an attorney who never showed up, he went insane waiting for hope and help. Eventually he made a stick man out of two slices of baloney, a paper cup, and some plastic spoons. Think of the movie *Cast Away*, where the protagonist Tom Hanks survived a plane crash in the South Pacific and lived on a deserted island for five years. In a test of extreme psychological torment, Tom Hanks invents an imaginary friend out of a washed-up soccer ball. He painted a face on it with his own blood and named the ball Wilson. Wilson became his best friend. Rooster did the same thing with his only friend whom he named Baloney Man.

One day in his boredom and eventual insanity, he decided to tie himself up with his jumpsuit and got caught in an awkward position. Fear overtook him. With his ankles and hands tied behind his back, he started crying uncontrollably, lost his bladder, and could not figure out how to get himself untied. Hours passed, and eventually a prison guard saw him lying on the floor in distress. He called other guards to help. They burst into his little concrete cage to untie him. Then the guards demanded, "Who did this to you?"

Confused and afraid, Rooster looked over in the corner of his cell where Baloney Man stood, and he said, nodding, "He did it."

After seven long, mundane years, the warden finally decided Rooster had enough of solitary, and he let him back into the prison population. Unfortunately, Rooster lost all his good time, picked up another charge, but then he finished his prison sentence. He left for a few months before he was back in prison on a parole violation. That is when I met him as a more subdued person. He lived in lethargy from antipsychotics, antidepressants, and sleeping aids. His joy came from the two times each day when he briskly waled to pill line to collect his daily doses of medicine. Sadly, prison life had left him and so many others in a zombie state where little of nothing was accomplished and life was wasted.

Hanging onto Hope

Someone has said that the hardest part of faith is the last half hour or last part of waiting. We tend to give up when relief is almost in sight. I am so weak sometimes that I feel like I am an expert at this. The English preacher Charles Spurgeon once said, "The wilderness is the way to Canaan. Defeat prepares us for victory. The darkest hours of the night precedes the dawn."[3] I know it sounds strange, but God wants to use this waiting place to change us, make us better, and help us accelerate in our faith. William Cowper, who wrote the wonderful hymn, "God Works in Mysterious Ways," explained, "The path of sorrow, and that path alone, leads to the place where sorrow is unknown."[4]

Our enemies want us to believe that this waiting place, as harsh as it may be, is a wasted place. Satan wants us to believe that our lives count for nothing and that we are not worth redemption. We deserve no more second chances. We all know what it feels like to be known by a number while our names are banished. We become forgotten, abandoned, and placed as far away from civilization as possible. We are invisible and unredeemable in society's eyes. By God's grace, we must constantly practice forgiveness and love toward those who desire our demise. We must always reject vengeful thoughts. Satan wants us to believe that we are wasted. We are no good. We are completely damaged goods with no possible value. But God says, "I have a plan for you…'For I know the plans that I have for you,' declares the Lord, 'plans for good and not for calamity to give you a future and a hope.'"[5]

Let me share a possible vision for us. If you are like me, you often feel unworthy to be used by God. But, from where we are right now, we can affect our world in ways that the angry, bitter, hostile, and resentful person can never do. With a cleansed heart that has no unresolved anger or conflict toward any other person, a life-changing connection with God is possible. Spurgeon says our devotion to God is the key to our promotion.[6]

God wants to move us from a life of chains to a life of spiritual prosperity. Listen to the psalmist, "God makes a home for the lonely; He leads out the prisoners into prosperity."[7] God wants prison to be a place of new beginnings. Our minds can move from being disorganized and irrational to being intelligent, creative, and disciplined. God can change everything about us. God is looking for people who are humble and broken enough to admit their mistakes, refuse to make excuses, and fully acknowledge His power and rightful place in our lives.

I know what it is like to be way too busy for God. Prior to 2011, I used to begin every day in quiet and stillness before God, but then I lost my peace in a busyness of irrational activity that eventually led to a complete barrenness. I could not concentrate on the present moment. Now I recognize once again that the past is irrecoverably gone and even the future is irrelevant. This present moment represents the intersection of eternity with time. I must make the most of it. Walter Wink says, "History belongs to the intercessors."[8]

Our lives do not have to be wasted. This waiting place does not have to be a wasted place because we can draw near to God and experience His presence. We can call upon the Lord, move upward in obedience, and fast-track our faith. He will show us what books to read, how to change our thinking, and what educational programs to pursue. It all starts with prayer.

Becoming a Prayer Warrior

Prayer changes your atmosphere. It takes the focus off your pain and pleasures and puts it on God. God becomes your pleasure. S. D. Gordon said, "The greatest thing anyone can do for God and man is pray. It is not the only thing; but it is the chief thing. The great people of the earth today are the people who pray. I do not mean those who talk about prayer; nor those who say they believe in prayer; nor yet those who can explain about prayer; but I mean those people who take time to pray."[9]

I have been in some of the deepest, darkest tunnels of depression and hopelessness. I have had to wrestle in prayer with God, and other times I have wondered where He was. Disappointment took over. Looking back, I now think of this painful period the way St. John of the Cross explained, "the dark night of the soul," or as Henri Nouwen talked about "the ministry of absence." A. W. Tozer described painful and lonely times as "the ministry of the night." Someone else called it the "winter of the heart." God takes all of His children through pain. Just like He gave us physical pain sensors to protect us from physical harm, He gives us painful things to cause us to draw closer to Jesus. C. S. Lewis tells us that pain is God's megaphone. It is God's way of arousing spiritual lethargy. Problems are not punishment; they are wake-up calls from a loving God. In God's absence, I would think of Isaiah's words, "The Lord has hidden Himself from His people."[10] There have been so many moments, especially in the past five years, when I yelled and screamed at God in anger and rage. I cried just like Jacob in the most desperate moment of his life, "God, I will not let you go until you bless me."[11] You have probably felt the same way. Maybe you have been bound by addictions. Maybe you have broken all relationships with the people you love and need, and you are now all alone. Maybe your health is a mess. Maybe you are beaten down by a life of failure and addiction. You need God's grace. You need a lift out of this pit of darkness.

> I waited patiently for the Lord; He turned to me and heard my cry. He lifted me out of the slimy pit, out of the mud and mire; He set my feet on a rock and gave me a firm place to stand. (Ps. 40:1)

E. M. Bounds, who has written eight books on prayer emphasizes, "Prayer is the channel though which all good flows to men. Prayer is a privilege, a sacred, princely privilege. Prayer is a duty, an obligation most binding, and most imperative, which should hold us to it. But prayer is more than a privilege, more than a duty. It is the appointed condition of getting God's aid. It is the avenue through which God supplies man's wants."[12]

Robert McCheyne said, "What a man is, he is alone on his knees before God and no more." Prayer is turning the soul to God. It is intimate communication with the Father. It is drawing close to God. You and I are being repotted for new growth and new beginnings. Incarceration must be seen as a new beginning, a turning of ourselves to God. Think of what the apostle Paul said while he was in prison, "Now I want you to know, brethren, that my circumstances have turned out for the greater progress (advancement) of the gospel." [13]

Prison is a waiting place, but prison does not have to be a wasted place. We are to bloom where God plants us. Our devotion to God will be our promotion. This waiting place can become the greatest place where God has ever placed us. We can pray, and when we pray, God acts. Not one minute is wasted when we pray. When we pray, we connect and communicate with God. We become more and more aware or conscious of His presence. It is impossible to yield in God's presence and not prosper. God becomes the center of our world. Every word, action, and thought is directed by Him, and His power in us.

I close this chapter by sharing two of my favorite verses on prayer given by God to a prophet who witnessed the desolation of his homeland.

> Call unto Me, and I will answer you, and I will tell you great and mighty things which you do not know. (Jer. 33:3)
>
> Then you will call upon Me and come and pray to Me, and I will listen to you. You will seek Me and find Me when you search for Me with all your heart. (Jer. 29:12–13)
>
> The greatest tragedy in life is not unanswered prayer; but unoffered prayer. (F. B. Myer)

Prayer: "Oh God, because You are with me, and because it is Your will that I knit my heart to Yours, I beg You by Your mercy to assist me with Your grace that I might call upon You continually and live in your presence. Dwell within my heart with all your peace and fullness."

Questions for reflection/discussion:
1. What does it mean to not waste the waiting time?
2. What are some life goals that you believe God wants you to accomplish while you are incarcerated?
3. Name some positive ways you can affect your family, associates, and world even while you are incarcerated?
4. How do you plan to overcome quitting points while you are in prison?
5. Explain what was unique about Nelson Mandela's release from prison after twenty-seven years of unjust confinement?
6. What can you do to improve yourself and please God in this very moment of time?

Chapter 2: Waiting Time

Lord, I wait for You; You will answer, Lord my God.
  —Psalms 38:15

There are no unanswered prayers. God answers yes, no, and not yet. Most prayers are answered with God saying, "Wait." Waiting means to rest, abide, dwell, trust, and believe. Patience is the capacity to endure without murmuring, complaining, and disillusionment. Patience means no condemning, no cussing, no railing others, and no blame. I belong to God, and I trust Him. He is working all things together for my good. In spite of this fiery oven He has placed me in, in all things I can give thanks. Waiting is not just passing time. It is prayer. The Psalms are a book of prayers. Do not just read them. Pray the psalms and make them part of your prayers too.

Marie

While waiting in jail, my daughter sent me the inspiring story of the heartbreaking and unjust incarceration of Marie Durant. In the late sixteen hundreds, the French Huguenots were under severe persecution for their Christian faith. Marie's story took place during the French civil wars between the Protestants and Catholics following the Reformation period that began with Martin Luther and other key figures. In 1685, French king Louis XIV reinstated Catholicism as the only authorized religion in France. Persecution of Protestants began again, and in 1715, Marie Durant was born. At the same time, King Louis XIV died. The next king, Louis XV, was even more draconian in his persecution of the Protestants.

    The Protestant Huguenots were not allowed to flee the country, so they met in secret. At fifteen years of age, Marie's parents were arrested and later died in prison. Her brother was also arrested and sentenced to death. Marie married a Huguenot pastor who himself was arrested and eventually killed. Marie was also arrested and placed in prison because she would not recant her faith.

    Placed in the infamous Tower of Constance in Southern France, she and other female prisoners were kept in an upper room with very little light and deplorable conditions. Inscribed on the wall of the tower is the slogan *Ja Resister*, meaning, "I resist." The authorities continually promised her freedom if she would recant her faith, but she never would. It was reported that while she was there, she read psalms, sang songs of worship, and was a great encouragement to other women in prison with her. She found comfort in memorizing the psalms. Finally, in 1767, after almost thirty-eight years of this cruel confinement, laws changed, and her obscenely unjust and sadistically inspired sentence was reversed. She was released and began a new life outside the tower walls. Her family was dead, and she lived another nine years in freedom before she passed away.[1]

    The story of Marie Durant is both sad and, at the same time, inspiring to me. How did she endure all that time of confinement? Were there times she felt abandoned and forsaken by God? How did it affect her sanity and mental capabilities? What happened to her IQ? What about her health and her eyesight? Were French authorities ever held accountable for this and other horrific atrocities? We may never know, as there is not much recorded history of her life. We do know that she made it, and that she used the book of Psalms more than any other book for her comfort and help.

    Sometimes we wait and patiently pray, and it seems that God is not listening. Believe me when I say I know what it feels like to see my faith grow weary. We often pray, and the answer we want does not come. We believe, but His promises appear to come up empty. In reality, we wonder why we have to wait so long. What is God doing? The battle for our faith intensifies, and at times, it seems that God is too busy or nowhere to be found. Why the absence? We wrongly believe He is not paying attention to us. Our spirits grow weary in what seems to be a never-ending waiting game of hide-and-seek.

    The writer of Hebrews explains that without faith it is impossible to please God.[2] Jude 25 is a prayer of honesty: "God have mercy on those who doubt." Doubts and questions will always come, but I think of doubt as a poison to block my faith. Often the poison comes through a negative or cynical inmate. Many prisoners believe there is no reason to even try and get better or try to fight their case for a way out of prison early. I am repeatedly told that I should just give up, escape by getting high, and quit worrying about it.

We must always be quick to reject wrong thinking. I believe that God wants to give us His favor. He is looking to and fro throughout the earth for whom He will bless. When others bitterly curse God in profane disrespect, we should praise God. When we hear God's name cursed, we should give Him praise. God inhabits the praise of His people. Hateful people will always abound. When others say we are stuck in here forever and that we are going to die in here, we must keep exercising our faith. When I hear negative rhetoric, it is an instant reminder to keep praying and not give up. I pray, "Lord, open doors for me that I might walk in Your path."

Accelerate in Your Faith While You Wait

The seas rarely part instantly. The giants do not always fall with the first stone, no matter how precise, accurate, and how much due diligence has been done. Our dreams and hopes may take years of patience as it did for Abraham and Sarah, who waited for the Promised Seed for almost eighty years (Gen. 15). We read in the New Testament, some two thousand years after Abraham, the apostle Paul explained that Abraham did not waiver in his faith as he waited. Waiver means he did not get discouraged or sidetracked from God's promise. Paul writes to the Roman Christians, "Yet, with respect to the promise of God, he did not waiver in unbelief, but *grew stronger* in his faith" (emphasis added).[3] He accelerated in his faith while waiting on God.

We can do the same. There is no need to waste even a minute of our time in prison. A long human life is 650,000 hours, and we all know that survival in prison is a tricky business, but God does not want us to simply survive. He wants us to thrive in Him. Moses prayed, "Lord, teach us to number our days that we might present to You a heart of wisdom."[4] We can set daily, weekly, monthly, and yearly goals integrated to our life of prayer or abiding in Christ. As an imprisoned pastor of Hitler, Dietrich Bonhoeffer wrote, "A day without morning and evening prayers and personal intercessions is actually a day without meaning and importance."[5]

No goal, dream, or desire lies out of our reach except that which is out of the will of God. There is no need to fear, and there is no need to give up. Reject all fatalism. We may vent our accumulated grief and frustration. We may sink in our sorrows at times, but we must never quit pursuing our God. One of my sons sent me a powerful quote while I was in jail. It said, "Sometimes the difference in history's boldest accomplishments and most staggering defeats is simply the diligent will to persevere."[6] Patience is the capacity to endure or persevere. It means we keep praying even when we don't feel like it. We keep pounding the doors of heaven, demonstrating belief that nothing is impossible with our God. The world may say we are forgotten and forsaken. They may want us to stay invisible and gone forever, but God is always working in our lives to draw us to Him, change us for His glory, and keep us walking with him. We must keep our prayers honest. We must keep our prayers simple. But we must keep on praying. My former pastor used to say to me often, "Keep on keeping on!" Don't give up!

> He has regarded the prayer of the destitute and has not despised their prayer. (Ps. 102:17)

Christmas in Prison

It was Christmas time and my first year in prison. I had received my apparent death sentence, and two months later, I was in another dreadful place. The prior two months I had received the diesel-therapy tour, being transported to a couple of different county jails and other federal holdovers. It was nothing but added dehumanization and depression. The prison I was at was built over one hundred years earlier, and it reminded me of some kind of ancient dungeon. Everything was dirty, old, and decrepit. My new friend, Charlie Red, and I were placed in a roach-infested cell where we would have to stay locked down twenty-three seven for the next two to four weeks. I did not want to touch anything. Because of my experience with solitary confinement, I began to hyperventilate in my spirit. Anxiety and restlessness took over. I asked Red to pray with me that God would help us. We prayed.

Thirty minutes later the head officer randomly came to our cell and asked us if we would work as orderlies. Charlie Red was experienced in doing time, and on the basis of his advice, we said yes. I did not realize it, but because we were orderlies, we were allowed to stay out of the cell, eat extra food, use the phone, e-mail our families, and stay busy. God answered our prayers almost immediately. I was reminded in that moment that God does nothing except in response to prayer. Prayer is everything.

Working as an orderly meant serving three hundred other inmates food trays for each meal through the food slots in the heavy steel doors among many other cleaning responsibilities. I worked from 6:00 a.m. until 9:00 p.m. each day for the next two weeks. I cleaned toilets, showers, mopped, waxed and buffed floors, pulled trash, did laundry, and served food trays. I was thankful for the job, but very tired after each day. My feet quickly bruised from improper footwear on the hard concrete. They swelled up from the pounding. At night, I stuck my red and swollen feet in a small trash can full of ice.

While working I got to meet many different inmates of all security classifications from many parts of the country and world. Most of the stories were sad. My heart sank many times as I heard and felt their regrets. Some were sick, some sad, and yes, some stories were plain evil and sadistic.

One inmate had a severe toothache, and I felt compassion for him. Medical treatment and dental care in prison is scant. One of the most common physical ailments in jail is the toothache. I had spent the prior six months battling an infected toothache only to be put off time and time again and given no help except the occasional Tylenol and a small cup of salt. It was like going to hell and asking for a friend. It was not going to happen. There were nights that the tooth pain was so intense that my mind went blank. The pain would bounce off my toes and back to the crown of my head like a ping-pong ball hour after hour.

This individual, a large burley fellow, was in so much pain he was begging me to get the dentist or some medicine for him. No medical staff came to help on that day, and he continued in agonizing pain. I had two Tylenols that I was saving for my own tooth pain. When I sensed God's prompting, I knew a step of obedience on my part would be required. God led me to do two things. I prayed that God would absorb his pain with His healing presence, and I gave him my last two Tylenols. I did the possible, and I trusted God to do the impossible.

Early the next morning, I was cleaning an empty cell after some inmates were transferred out in the middle of the night. When I pulled back the sleeping mat, there it was. Left behind was a brand-new bottle of one hundred Tylenols. I immediately remembered that we could not outgive God. I gave thanks to God, and I was able to share with others with similar pains. Later that night my friend said, "Thanks, bud. What can I do to repay you?"

I said, "Nothing. Consider it a gift from Jesus."

I remember something that Dwight L. Moody once wrote, "Out of one hundred men, one will read the Bible, the other ninety-nine will read the Christian."[7] St. Francis of Assisi said, "Preach the gospel at all times, if necessary, use words."[8]

My daughter works in a hospital and serves people everyday. She is learning to become what Mother Teresa said while she was working with the most destitute people dying of AIDS and Leprosy in India. She said, "I am a pencil in the hand of God writing a love letter to the world."[9]

Prayer changes everything. Our focus cannot be on changing laws, but changing lives.

Consider the English missionary George Muller. He was a man of dedicated prayer and sacrificial service to the Lord. In the eighteen hundreds God used him to feed thousands of orphan children at times when he had nothing at all to give. He woke up every day aware of this great need for God's intervention, and throughout his life, he documented some fifty thousand answered prayers. He is famous for saying, "God does nothing except in response to prayer."[10] The apostle James tells us, "The fervent prayer of a righteous man avails much." We pray with persistence (the fervent prayer). We pray with confidence—the righteous man has the favor of God (Ps. 5:12). And we pray with faith.

D. L. Moody explained, "I would rather pray like David than preach with the elegance of Gabriel." He went on, "I felt guilty if I heard the blacksmith hammering before I was praying."[11]
It is hard to get up early, but Moody got up early. He prayed. His destiny was determined by the early daylight hours. Intimate connection with God changes everything.

God is infinitely powerful and able to do far more than we could ever ask or think (Eph. 3:20). God has brought us to this place of helplessness so that we fully comprehend that He is all we need. He is not absent. He has not abandoned us. He has not left us. We may have left him. We may have walked in disbelief and followed our own desires. As we open our spiritual eyes, turn from our sins, and practice His presence, we experience God. Prayer and fasting unlock all dead bolts. Those who wait on the Lord will renew their strength.[12]

Waiting on God is not wasted time. While we are praying, seeking and obeying God, our faith is growing. The act of waiting builds qualities of patience, love, persistence, trust, gentleness, and compassion. By waiting on God, we are always on an upward spiritual path of progress and prosperity. Prayer builds positive energy!

Prayer: "Lord, help me. I am in need. Help me be still before You. Help me stop worrying and trust You. You are my refuge and strength, a present help in time of trouble. Amen."

Questions for reflection/discussion:
1. What does it mean to pray fervently?
2. Name some ways you can measure spiritual growth and progress while you wait on God.
3. What dreams, goals, and visions are out of the Christians' reach?
4. Describe the specific actions Marie Durant took to help others while she waited on God in prison.
5. How does prayer fulfill the great commandment to love God with all your heart, soul, and mind?

When one walks lovesick for God, he is at the heights of prayer life, and he is fulfilling the great commandment to perfection.
—St. John of the Cross[13]

Chapter 3: A New Day

Prayer: "God. Make me new. Help me forget my past failures. Remake me. Repot me in fresh soil. Free me from these chains of the flesh, worldly pursuits and intellectual confinement. Redirect me on an upward spiritual path."

Some people have terrible things happen to them. My jovial friend Bobby, a.k.a. as Lucky, lost his arm the night of his father's funeral. After he buried his dad, in his depression, he went to the local bar and got drunk. At about midnight he attempted to walk six blocks to the place where he was staying. In a drunken stupor, he became disoriented and passed out underneath a train boxcar on the railroad tracks. Several hours later the train began to move, severing his arm at his shoulder (which lay helplessly over the railroad tracks) and then ripping off his jacket. When he tried to sit up, the metal railroad car knocked out his front teeth, split his lips, and left him laid out for dead. In amazing persistence and determination, he got up and stumbled to someone's front door who called for help. His arm and jacket were found two hundred miles away in Ft. Smith, Arkansas. Not much later, depression from a tough life dug in deeper. In Jacksonville, Florida, he drank a glass of antifreeze to kill himself. His organs shut down, and he spent the next week in a coma and on dialysis before surviving again. His life of petty crime, alcoholism, and drug use to deaden the emotional and psychological pain has so far cost him thirteen years in prison, all on the installment plan, and he is only in his midthirties. He still struggles with the demons of addiction and abuse.

When I met him in the dreadful county jail, he was arrested for pawning his brother's lawn mower so he could pay for a bag of dope and time with a prostitute. Since being incarcerated, I have heard hundreds of similar stories of the many mistakes made with the seductive woman and the relentless power that sexual temptation has over a man. Marriages are destroyed. Trust is broken. Assaults are committed.

We want to escape the pain of prison, bad relationships, and unresolved conflicts. But just like God uses sensory pain in our lives to warn us and to protect us from sharp objects, fire, freezing temperatures, objects of blunt force, and the fear of falling down, so

God uses the emotional and psychological pain as a warning sign. He wants to protect us from the negative consequences of sin.

He also uses pain to enhance pleasure. After my first twenty-one days of solitary confinement and two paltry meals a day in the county jail, almost anything tastes good. Ecstasy replaces the agony of constant hunger pain. In jail, I went from 167 pounds to 143 pounds and learned that hunger is by far the best seasoning. Even stale white bread, cheap baloney, and pink boiled hot dogs, items I never ate before, taste good in jail. St. Augustine writes of this same idea, "Everywhere a greater joy is preceded by a greater suffering."

My long time cellie and good friend, Terry Buck, tells the story of how he was cheating on his "old lady," as she caught him on the phone with his mistress. In a fit of rage and jealousy, she verbally assaulted him and cursed him from behind their trailer. He got so mad at her that he threw the cell phone from what he says was at least fifty feet. He never believed he would hit her directly between the eyes. She cried in agony, called the sheriff, and would not wipe away the oozing blood that covered her face and front of her shirt until the police came to take pictures and make the report. They took Buck away in handcuffs. The next morning in court, the Judge asked Buck, "What the hell is wrong with you?"

Buck said, "Your Honor, you could give me every cell phone in North Carolina and give me as many free throws at my wife from the same distance, and I could never hit her between the eyes again. It was a freak accident." The judge did not believe him and gave him another eighteen months in state prison for domestic assault.

From Death to Life

In chapter 8 of the book of John, we find a story of a woman who was caught in the act of adultery. Adultery is the commission of sex outside of the relationship of marriage. Jesus had already explained that looking upon another person to lust after him or her in the heart is the same as committing adultery.[1] Nonetheless, under the Old Testament Law, the penalty for adultery was death by stoning. While it takes two to commit the actual act of adultery, this woman alone was driven to the place of Jesus by the Pharisees and religious leaders. Their hope was to destroy this woman and catch Jesus in some kind of theological trap to discredit Him.

The religious leaders of that day were driven by money, power, and influence. Their religion was a dead, mechanical system that used fear and greed to make money and keep power and control of their religious society. Jesus was seen as a major impediment to their system. The greater the holiness, the greater the hostility. Yet, the masses were drawn to Jesus's compassion, grace, and supernatural wisdom. He had driven the money changers out of the temple, and they wanted Jesus eliminated because He was bad for business. He healed on the Sabbath to show how bad the religious leaders had misinterpreted the Old Testament, while they intentionally kept the common person and the poor in bondage and oppression. Instead of taking advantage of people, Jesus came on the scene and extended amazing grace to ordinary people who had little hope. He loved the unloved and gave those with no hope value and vision. Jesus always sees everyone through the lens of second chances.

The Pharisees devised a plan to have Jesus arrested, and they hoped that Jesus would not know how to handle the problem of this woman caught in adultery. If Jesus agreed to have this woman be stoned, the people might have withdrawn from Him and certainly believed He was too harsh. On the other hand, if Jesus said, "Let her go," it would be clear that Jesus would be defying the law. He would be seen as too lenient, and it would show that God is a pushover and that we humans can sin and get away with it. The philosophy of antinomianism believes that we can sin and do all the wrong we want and then simply ask God to forgive us and keep repeating the same sins over and over again with no consequences. Some people commit sin and think that they are getting away with it, but it is impossible. As the great preacher R. G. Lee proclaimed, "[T]here is always a pay day some day."[2] God knows all our sins, and every sin has a built-in negative consequence.

As I have lived longer, I realize how much God's commandments make sense. Everything is for our good. God is not out there to spoil our fun or ruin our good time. He wants to protect us, and the commandments are like guardrails to keep us from falling off the cliff.

The purpose of the devious plan of the Pharisees was to discredit Jesus, but Jesus turned their scheme around on them. He knew she already had been publicly shamed and humiliated for her sin. The punishment was more than enough for her, and Jesus clearly understood there was a limit to how much punishment should be inflicted on anyone's transgression. Punishment is needed for those who break laws, sadly though, most prisoners are punished far more than the true nature of their crimes.

Instead of passing judgment on the woman, Jesus passed judgment on the Pharisees. He was outraged at how quickly they would condemn another person but not take time to judge themselves. He decided to help them out with identifying their own sins. They asked Him, "The Law says to stone such a woman; what then do you say" (John 8:5)? The next verse says Jesus stooped down and with His finger wrote on the ground. What did He write? Judging from the response of the Pharisees, it had to be significant as everyone quickly and quietly cleared out.

Throughout history, man has speculated at what He wrote. Obviously, He was not just scribbling in the dirt. He could have written some other scriptures. He could have written down the secret sins of each of the Pharisees who were all appearing to be someone they were not. They could not fool God. He knows every secret thought and internal motive of our life for all of time. In Psalms 139:1–4, David prayed,

> O Lord, You have searched me and known me. You know when I sit down and when I rise up; You understand my thoughts from afar. You scrutinize my path and my lying down, and are intimately acquainted with all my ways. Even before there is a word on my tongue, behold, O Lord, You know it all.

God knows everything about us. That is why David prayed in Psalms 19:12, "Who can discern his errors? Acquit me of secret faults." Then again, in Psalms 26:2, "Examine me, oh Lord, and try me; test my mind and my heart." In Romans 2:16, the apostle Paul explains to us that "on the day when according to my gospel, God will judge the secrets of men through Jesus Christ." You see, there are no secrets with God. Secret sin on earth is open scandal in heaven.

He Who Is Without Sin

Can you imagine each of these Pharisees standing there reading what He wrote? It had to be about their personal sin. Jesus then said, "He who is without sin, cast the first stone (v. 7)." Now that their sins and their secret motives to slander and kill this woman had been revealed, they all walked away. When they all left, Jesus said to the woman, "Woman, where are they? Did no one condemn you (v. 10)?" Note that Jesus called her "Woman." In that culture, it was a term of endearment and respect. She was not used to being treated with respect and kindness, but that is how Jesus treats people. Grace pours through all His words. There is no one like Jesus. She had been looked down upon by society in many ways, but Jesus elevated her to a whole new level of confidence. He gave her life when just minutes before she was facing a most brutal and harsh death.

It is important to understand that God does not look at us the way the world does. We all have been told that because we are incarcerated, we are hopeless losers. It often seems like everyone highlights our shortcomings and mistakes. The government and all prison and jail officials magnify, every day of our lives, our mistakes. Playing the role of Satan, the accuser, they make sure we never forget them.

My parents came to see me not long ago at my prison in South Carolina. The correctional officer who escorted me to the visitation room knew nothing about me, and I had never spoken to him before. He did not even know my name, but he proceeded to take the opportunity to belittle and bemoan my shortcomings. He said, "Your people have come to see you today, and you should be thankful. I would never come see my children if they were in here. They wouldn't deserve it. This is a real privilege for you, young man. You live in here with three good meals, clothes, a roof over your head, while they are out there slaving, paying taxes, and struggling to get by. I hope you remember this next time you decide to break the law." I did not even respond to his comments. It is part of the cruel and unredemptive environment of one-size-fits-all punishment.

We don't have to look in the mirror to see and realize our own flaws. We are reminded of them everyday. But God looks at us and sees what He can make of us. He sees what we can be, what He can make us into, and the grace-giving potential of our lives. He looks in our hearts. He knows our struggles with temptation.

Not long ago I saw a transvestite prisoner sit down by himself, shunned as usual. He sat up straight, brushed his long hair back out of his eyes, and bowed his head to pray. I could tell even from a distance that he was very humble and sincere. I was moved in my spirit to reach out to him even knowing that I would have problems with other prisoners. Surprisingly, he was very open to discussing Christ and quietly admitted he was very confused and in need of help. We must see people the way Jesus sees them.

A Pitiful Wretch

Everyone else saw the woman caught in adultery as a sinner—a pitiful wretch living an immoral life. Soren Kierkegaard said, "Once you label me, you neglect me."[3] But with a few shocking words of amazing grace, Jesus changed her life. He said, "Neither do I condemn you. Go and sin no more." Perhaps, for the first time in her life, she lifted her eyes, and instead of gazing into the sharp and narrow eyes of a harsh and uncaring judge, she looked into the very eyes of God. Instead of scorn and hatred, she saw eyes that burned with a deep love and tender compassion. Jesus did not say, "Go and live a perfect and flawless life, and maybe later, I will forgive you." If He did, none of us would ever be forgiven. We would have no hope. If the Lord marked our iniquities, who could stand?[4] Jesus said, "Neither do I condemn you. Go and sin no more."

Jesus's act of forgiveness and grace was followed by the challenge: "Go and sin no more." Why? Because if you keep on sinning, something much worse will come upon you.[5] If the evil spirit finds the house empty and swept clean, seven more will enter with it. We must fill the empty spaces where sin ruled. We must replace the old with the new. The bottom line is that there needs to be a change in our behavior. If not, God may send leanness of the soul or the inability to know Him intimately (Ps. 106:15).

Sin is costly. Just as this woman was pardoned from her sins, Jesus would soon go to the cross to pay for her sins, ours sins, and the sins of the entire world. Forgiveness may seem free, but it is not cheap. It cost God separation from His beloved Son. While it can't be earned or worked for ("lest any man boast" [Eph. 2:10]), it also comes with a price. Imprisoned World War II German pastor Dietrich Bonhoeffer explained, "Grace is free, but it is not cheap."[6] God loves to give second chances and grant forgiveness and grace, but He demands our loyalty and devotion.

Every day in prison, our prison sentence reports are the first thing any correctional officer or counselor reads. Some of them like referring to our past sins and mistakes. They want to know what we did to get in here. The system we are bound by naturally causes daily condemnation. But note this fact about the ministry of Christ: Jesus never talks about the past. He only talks about the present and the future. The past is gone. We cannot live in the past. Justification by faith in Christ means that we are viewed as though we have never sinned.[7]

Not only does God forgive but He also forgets the past. Listen to Jeremiah 31:34, "I will forgive their wickedness and will remember their sins no more." Psalms 103:12 says, "I will remove their sins as far as the east is from the west." One of the most important verses of Christian theology is Romans 8:1. It says, "There is no condemnation for those who are in Christ Jesus."

An unknown fourteenth-century Englishman wrote a book called *The Cloud of Unknowing*, which became a classic about how to communicate with God. He said that before penetrating the cloud of unknowing above us in prayer, we needed to imagine a cloud of forgetting beneath us. The idea is that we clear our minds, forget all the condemnation of our past sins, and fill up with the truth and glory of God. We must forget past failures, recurring sins, and feelings of inferiority and condemnation. Instead, open your mind to God. He will not fill what has not been emptied.

The devil, the media, the government, the Internet age, and the world hate this idea. They love to bring up our past mistakes as often as they can. They love to hit the "play over" button until we sink in despair. They want us to keep looking in the rearview mirror. They love to remind us of our past. But God forgives. Justification is not only about what God takes away (our sin) but also about what He puts in its place. He instantly imputes or credits righteousness to those who trust Him by faith. The books are now balanced. With Christ's righteousness now ours, there is no condemnation. There is no need to fear death and face God on Judgment Day.

This woman went from being stoned to death and exiting the world to living a new and full life on earth with eternal confidence in His perfect righteousness. Jesus invites us to do the same. My experience is that I can do nothing better than abandon myself to God, blessing God, praising God, adoring God, giving Him the love of my whole heart.

Prayer: "Lord Jesus. I realize I am a sinner in need of Your mercy. Forgive me. Come into my heart. Be my Lord and Savior. Thank you for saving me."

> To pray is to mount on eagle's wings above the clouds and get into the clear heaven where God dwells. To pray is to enter the treasure house of God's and to enrich oneself out of an inexhaustible storehouse. To pray is to grasp heaven in one's arms, to embrace the Diety within one's soul, and to feel one's body made a temple of the Holy Ghost. (Charles H. Spurgeon)[8]

Questions for reflection/discussion:
1. Why did the Sadducees and Pharisees wish to discredit Jesus and catch Him in a theological trap?
2. What is the philosophy of antinomianism, and why is it not biblical? Cross-reference: Romans 6:1–2.
3. Why is it impossible to love people if we are judging and condemning them?
4. Describe what R. G. Lee meant when he said there was a payday someday. Cross-reference: Galatians 6:7.
5. Why do you think Jesus never refers to the past but only the present and the future? Cross-reference: Philippians 3:13–14.

When I consider Your heavens, the work of Your fingers the moon and the stars, which You have ordained, what is man that You take thought of him, and the son of man that You care for him?
—Psalms 8:3–4

Chapter 4: A Starting Point for Change

One of my best friends and cell mates was a man I will call Chuck. At age four, his father died. At age five, his mother died. He was raised by his grandmother and older brothers. A couple of times, he attended a Baptist church, and at age eleven, he was baptized, although he says he only did it to make his grandmother happy. With little guidance through his adolescent years, he quit high school and quickly got in trouble with the law. Alcohol, cigarettes, and women were his main vices. One night he was drinking at the pool hall and got into a vicious fight over a girl. Afterward, he followed his assailant to his house, broke through the front door, and beat him with a baseball bat. He was charged with breaking and entering and aggravated assault. It was his first official charge.

He turned nineteen in state prison and was released one year later. Even though he was in prison, he found ways to drink his "prison made" alcohol and stayed addicted. When he was released, the probation department put him on Antabuse, a medicine that counteracts alcohol. The first night out of prison, he called his friends, went to the same pool hall, and got drunk. He told me that, the next three days, he was curled up in a fetal position sick from the Antabuse. He said, "I thought I was going to die."

The next thirteen years, he flew fairly straight with only a few overnight jail stints and worked as a car mechanic and as a driver of a Dr. Pepper delivery truck. He never got married, but he had two long-term relationships with women he called his "old ladies." He has one child with each one. At age thirty-two, he discovered heroin. It was all down hill from there. Life spiraled quickly out of control as he spent every spare dollar on his ever-growing habit. He collected multiple traffic violations, forty-nine to be exact, many of which were simple repeat offenses of driving with a suspended license. One day he was pulled over by the state patrol and decided to make a run for it instead of going to jail. He fled through a field to get away because his license was revoked. Winded from years of smoking, Chuck was quickly caught by the state patrolman in a muddy field. The state patrolman said, "Boy! What are you running for? Did you rob a bank or something?"

Chuck said, "No. My license is revoked."

The patrolman asked, "You mean to tell me I had to chase you down and got my boots all dirty over a suspended license?"

Chuck said, "Yes, sir."

Soon Chuck started picking up smaller charges of possession of stolen goods and domestic assault and did a couple more short-term stints in state prison. He served a total of about eight years, all on the installment plan. In and out of prison, he continued to use heroin. Heroin was everything to him. Heroin or some derivative is always available in prison. He told me, "I loved heroin more than Peter loved the Lord." Soon, heroin users and dealers became his only acquaintances. He told me many sad stories of those who died chasing the high from drug overdoses. Users and abusers would show up at his shop, sell him stolen equipment, and then he resold the goods at higher prices to support his own heroin habit. At age forty-six, he loved heroin more than life itself. His arms, legs, and toes have multiple track marks like I have never seen before. I asked him how he got such deep track marks on his arms, and he said, "Dope sick. I would be driving down the road and need a hit. I would pull out a syringe and just stab away until I found an open vein. I would be bleeding in multiple places, and the blood would just flow out." It was heroin that blinded him from having a part in the theft of twenty-three guns from a deceased man's home. He received a total of seventy-five dollars for his part, and that, along with his lengthy criminal history, got him nine long and harsh years in federal prison when he really needed a serious rehab program.

After my first thirty days in the BOP, Chuck became my cellie, my prayer partner, and my best friend in prison. Nonetheless, the addictions still had power over his body and memory. He had many fears and battled numerous insecurities. After forty years of addiction, I would silently ask God how he could ever change. How could he turn from this condemnation and defeat to a life of confidence? Where does he even start? For Chuck, temptation to use and abuse various drugs in prison was daily.

He and I began praying together, and I knew his heart was sincere. Sometimes when we turned the lights out after count, he would remind me to lead us in prayer. I would pray. He agreed with the prayer, and then he would meekly say, "Thank you." One night he reminded me to pray for my friend named Yvette who had cancer, when I had forgotten. We prayed again. I challenged him every week to write his children, and then, I would watch him labor in anguish with his GED education over various letters that he would send home. The rejection he felt over his status often overwhelmed him. His kids needed him, and he needed his kids.

Chuck tried hard to seek God while fighting past demons. He prayed prayers of salvation and worried over what would happen if he died. Not long ago he finished reading the entire New Testament for the first time in his life. He asked me a thousand questions along the way, and it blessed me to see his eyes light up as he began to put together a basic systematic theology. Even so, the memories of sin and sickness never left him. It bothered him deeply. His remorse and regret over his addictions, lost time with his family, and opportunities to do right were sincere.

How can he and I effect real, lasting change in our lives? Change means to be made different. It means to alter, modify, convert, and transform. In the Bible, the word "repent" is a strong word for change. "Repent" means to change the way we think about sin. It means to turn from yourself and turn to God. "Repent" means to change our thinking. We must see sin the way God sees it. Sin might be pleasurable for a season, but it always leads to death. Sin always hurts God, others, and ourselves with its built-in negative consequences. The Greek word *metanoia* means to change directions. It is related to the word "metamorphosis," which speaks of transformation.

Repentance

Repentance is not easy. It is not quick, and it is not painless. It does not speak of a slight change of thinking. Instead, it speaks of an about-face type of change in attitude and thought. Forsaking sin takes serious work. Discipline is required. Sacrifices have to be made. It means that we deal with deep, root issues of pride, selfishness, and bitterness. Real change is not like pulling weed tops. If we just pull the top of the weed and leave the root, it grows right back. In order for us to change, we must deal with the root problems and causes of our wrong thinking and behavior.

The apostle Paul said, "Be not conformed to this world, but be transformed by the renewing of your mind."[1] Change begins with the renewing of our minds. I began to teach Chuck that we should give each day back to God and start each day with a quiet time of prayer of at least thirty minutes. A quiet time is time alone with God. Below are five steps to a quiet time.

1. *Find a quiet place with as little distractions as possible.* Solitary time or time alone from other inmates is not easy in prison because privacy is almost nonexistent. Do the best you can to find that spot. You may have to have a conversation with your cellie and politely explain that, during certain times, you will be reading, meditating, and praying, and that you would appreciate not being disturbed unless it is an emergency. The idea is to be quiet and give the worries of each day to the Lord. I make my bunk a holy place. I pray over it. I dedicate it to the Lord. I give myself repeatedly to God every night before I go to sleep and when I wake up in the morning.

2. *Have a set time early in the day or morning.* David prayed, "Oh God, You are my God; I shall seek You earnestly; my soul thirst for You, my flesh yearns for You."[2] He also prayed, "As the deer pants for the water brooks, so my soul pants for You, oh God. My soul thirsts for God, for the living God."[3] I give God the first part of my day confessing my sins and allowing Him the opportunity to speak into my life. He gives me direction for my daily activities. Guard this quiet time with your life. Protect it. Jesus says, "But seek first His kingdom and His righteousness, and all these things will be added to you."[4] Exalting God to His proper place in my life allows Him to take care of all my problems. David proclaims, "Sit at my right hand, and I will make your enemies a footstool to my feet."[5] God wants to take care of all our problems. Sit at His feet. Sit at His right hand and trust Him.

3. *Make a reading plan.* Read and meditate on the Bible. Reading remains the best way to engage the world, keep your mind free, and understand life's most important questions. It will help you maintain sanity. I personally try to read five psalms (broken into thirty sections for each day of the month), one proverb (one for each day of the month), and at least three other chapters of the Bible to allow me to read through the entire Bible at least one time each year. There are many Bible reading plans out there. Find one you like and stay with it.

4. *Use a spiritual journal or blank notebook where you can make and keep a current prayer list.* Write down your prayer

requests, supplications, and petitions along with important dates and times so that you can keep track of how God is answering your prayers. Pray for your family, friends, loved ones, the sick, the poor, your enemies, authorities that God has placed over your life like your case manager, your counselor, other officers, wardens, your judge, your prosecutor, your probation officer, and other law enforcement officials. Pray for Congress, the Supreme Court, the president, the Department of Justice and those in the military. Pray for your hometown and your state. Pray for the victims of your crime and those you hope to reconcile with, whom you may have offended.

5. *Begin your time of prayer with quiet meditation and then move into a time of confession of sin.* Confess all known sin to the Lord. For me, this often takes some time. Ask God to cleanse your heart of all known and unknown sin. Forgive others of their sins against you. If you do not forgive, God will block your prayers. It is just that simple. Unforgiveness and bitterness are the surest ways for your prayers to be hindered. Remember there are no unanswered prayers; however, there are blocked prayers. Psalms 66:18 declares, "If I cherish iniquity in my heart, the Lord will not hear me." Isaiah 1:14–17 is another important passage that speaks of why we must be clean before we pray. Jesus makes it very clear in many gospel passages that if we do not forgive others, God will not forgive us. Our relationship with God is totally dependent on us forgiving others. Jesus says, "If you come to the altar (the meeting place of God-the place of prayer) and there remember you have a problem with your brother, leave your gift (or your prayer), go make things right and then come back and offer your prayer."[6] Remember that you will never be asked to forgive anyone any more than what God has already forgiven you.

Once you are clean and pure before God and others, you can boldly read, meditate, spend time in praise and worship, lift up requests, tell God your heart, beg and plead for His intervention, ask Him for guidance, for wants and needs, and intercede for others. We are to come boldly before His throne that we may obtain mercy and find grace to help in our time of need.[7] Intercession is the highest form of service to others. There is no greater act of mercy that you can perform for others than to labor for them in prayer. I will talk more about this in later chapters, but keep this thought in mind: great opportunities often disguise themselves in small mundane tasks that are unsought, unloved, and unrewarded by the world. However, God sees. He knows.

Brother Lawrence, a well-known seventeenth-century monk known for his intimate and personal walk with God, said, "I do not advise you to use a great multiplicity of words in prayer since long discourses are often occasions for wandering."[8] The place and practice of prayer is where all change happens.

> So when you spread out your hands in prayer, I will hide my eyes from you, yes even though you multiply prayers, I will not listen. Your hands are covered with blood. Wash yourselves, make yourselves clean; remove the evil of your deeds from My sight. Cease to do evil. (Isa. 1:15–16)

Question for reflection/discussion:
1. Define change.
2. What habits do you need to change?
3. What parts of having a quiet time are hardest for you to implement? Why?
4. How does a quiet time set the stage for each day?
5. Why is it so important to begin your day with a quiet time?
6. The quiet time should never be rushed or hurried. Why do you think this is true or not true?
7. Describe your commitment to spend time alone with God each day. Where will you meet Him? What time? For how long? What will you read? Whom and what will you pray for? What dreams and goals are on the top of your prayer list? What verses of scripture do you plan to meditate on and memorize?

Chapter 5: Peace with God

When Jesus spoke of following Him, He often referred to the cross. In Roman culture, the cross only meant one thing: suffering and death. The disciples clearly understood the culture in which they lived. Roman generals had conquered the entire world during the prior two centuries. Rome was the capital of the world with over one million residents. Latin and Greek were the primary languages spoken. The land of Judah and Galilee were taxed and ruled under Roman control with Roman-appointed governors, overseers, and military. Roman cities like Tiberius and Caesarea Philippi were well established in the land formerly known as Israel.

      The disciples or followers of Jesus saw legions of Roman soldiers live within and patrol their Roman territories. Bronze, silver, and gold denarius coins, which they used for money, had the Roman Caesar's image engraved on the daily-circulated metal. When anyone, slave or free, revolted against Rome, an angry Roman governor could quickly condemn the accused to death. After the condemned was stripped of his clothes, he was violently tied down, humiliated, and brutally beaten by strong-willed soldiers swinging leather laced with sharp pieces of metal designed to strip the flesh off the bone. The blood flowed freely.

      Once the unbearable flogging is complete, the rebellious or lawless subject is forced to carry the heavy cross to the place of execution. He would then be nailed through the hands and feet and hung on a wooden cross as an example to the public, where he moaned and begged for a quick death. Eventually, he would die. It was the most brutal, barbaric, cruel, and unusual method of punishment ever conjured up in the human mind. The Romans used it to deter crime and force submission to their rule. The cross was a permanent image of sadistic fear that no citizen of that time ever forgot.

Follow Me

Jesus told His disciples, "Follow Me."[1] Christianity is total adherence to the person of Christ. When one submits to Him as Savior and Lord, it is impossible not to change. While following Jesus means eternal life in heaven, it also means that while we are on earth, we must follow Him even though at times it means suffering and death. All who followed Christ, understood this, and certainly, they were afraid. They were scared.

The apostle Paul later explained by revelation of God in the book of Romans, "That if you confess with your mouth Jesus as Lord, and believe in your heart that God has raised Him from the dead, you will be saved."[2] To confess that Jesus is Lord, and not the Roman Caesar, meant to give allegiance to a different king than the caesar. It was punishable by death. If a Roman soldier demanded your confession to the Caesar as Lord, and you did not kneel but instead confessed Christ as Lord, even though King Jesus is of another world, it still meant a possible death sentence by crucifixion. The confession of Christ carried a lot of heavy responsibility, and after Christ, thousands of Christians would die upon the cross at the hands of the Romans.

I write all of this to explain that coming to Christ means living a radically different life, a changed life. It is not easy believism and cheap receivism. One cannot be a Christian without repentance from sin. Sin is breaking God's moral and divine law. It is intentionally and accidentally offending God. Everyone has offended God. There is none without sin.[3] There are many times when we have offended God, and we may not even be aware that we have offended Him. That is why David prayed, "Acquit me of hidden faults."[4]

Sin is disobeying God. It is ignoring God. It is choosing our own way over His way. It is living independent of God. Sin blocks our fellowship with God. Sin separates us from God. The word "transgression," a common word used for sin throughout the Bible, means to go beyond the limits set by God. Literally, to transgress means to miss the mark, like missing a target. We have all missed the mark or standard of perfect behavior required by God. No one has ever kept the Ten Commandments perfectly all their lives. We have all broken many of God's 613 Old Testament laws, and no one has perfectly kept the great commandments of always love God and always love your neighbor as yourself. Moreover, no one has perfectly fulfilled the great commission, which says to go into all the world and share the gospel to all peoples and all nations.

Another synonym or similar word used for sin is the word "iniquity." "Iniquity" means wrongful conduct. When we sin, no matter how big or small, we personally offend God. There is an unwritten code of conduct among prison inmates. The most important code to follow is to show respect, give space, and have tolerance for other inmate's beliefs, possessions, and private conversations. In essence, mind your own business. One of my fellow inmates says, "Prison is like walking barefoot through a den of rattlesnakes. You must tread lightly and stomp on a head when necessary." Some inmates get their heads stomped, and the most common reason for this is that someone has been disrespected or offended.

 Changing means that we conform to God's code of conduct as given to us through the Bible and the person of Christ. The Bible teaches that we are sinners by nature and choice. The first step to change is that we admit to God, others, and ourselves the exact or precise nature of our wrongs. We cannot make excuses or justify our wrong behavior. We must own or "man up" and accept responsibility for what we have done wrong. We will not truly begin the process of change or transformation until we address the defects of our character caused by our sin nature.

 To be clear, we must admit, agree with, or confess that we lied, stole, cheated, hurt, assaulted, murdered, caused pain, and offended God and others. We cannot expect God to forgive our sin until we have properly confessed our sin to God. Someone has said, "Calvary only covers what we uncover."

Finding My Way to Christ

Before I was a Christian at age seventeen, I thought at different times that I was always a Christian. I was a member of a church. I had been baptized. I attended church sometimes. My parents were Christians. I generally was a good person. One day a friend asked me the question, "When you became a Christian, did anything change about your life?" He showed me a verse in 2 Corinthians that says, "Therefore, if anyone is in Christ, he is a new creature; the old things passed away; behold, new things have come."[5]

 I thought about his question and realized that nothing had changed about my life. I still used the same old language, the same old thought processes, and still followed my same selfish ways. I did not pray. I did not worship. Yes, I showed up at worship services, but I never worshipped God with my heart. My mind was always someplace else. I never told God personally that I loved Him. I had no hunger or desire to know and understand God's Word, nor did I ever tell anyone else that I was a Christian. It was not part of my language or behavior. My life was mine to do as I pleased. There was no new awareness of right and wrong, or a desire to change old habits, language, or plans. My friend emphasized to me that if I was a Christian, my language and desires would be different, and I would want to love others and serve instead of always being served. He said I would also pray. A person who never prays, ever, cannot be a Christian. Prayer is the natural language of a child of God.

At that point, I began to think deeply about the sincerity of my relationship with God. It is possible that I was a very young and immature Christian. However, after a lengthy internal struggle, I converted to Christ and began a personal relationship with God. It was not a quick or hasty commitment. There were intolerable conflicts of my soul as my heart was fixed on sports, money, peers, and infatuation. I began to fear my wickedness and disobedience to God might be an unpardonable sin, and I began to understand that my sin had separated me from God. Eventually, I felt hopelessly doomed until I finally repented and surrendered myself to Him, who knew no sin but became sin for me that I might be saved.

It was not for show or to win some girl's heart or impress my parents, teachers, and friends. On June 20, 1983, I wandered into the woods, got down on my knees, and the best way I knew how, I committed my life into His hands. I repented of my sin. God began the work of sanctification in my life, which is the life-long process of change into the predestined image of Christ.

Did I become perfect? Hardly. If anything, I became more aware that I was even worse than I once feared. My faith, belief, trust in Christ alone and His grace, not my goodness, works, or personal efforts, but His righteousness alone, became my sole hope for eternal salvation. I was unworthy. He was worthy. I was unholy. He was holy. Jesus became my much-needed best Friend, Savior, and Lord. That is when I first began to pray and understand His love for me.

First and Lasts

Today on the compound, there is sad news. An inmate in solitary confinement committed suicide. For most, the pressure and burden of prison are so much beyond what the body and mind is meant to endure. I did not know this particular prisoner. I wish I had known him. Bob Pierce, founder of the global charity World Vision, says, "Lord, may my heart be broken by what breaks your heart."[6] My heart is sad for him and his family no matter what had happened in his past. Depression is a horrible monster. Dreams are over. Life on this earth is complete.

Which makes me think this: there are always firsts and lasts. There are beginnings and endings. There are first steps and a last step. There is a first breath and a last breath. There are introductions and good-byes. There are sunrises and sunsets. And there is a crib and a casket. When we leave this world, we leave all that we have, and what we take with us is all that we are—our character, our person. Our identity is to be consumed in Christ.

> The birds on the branch, the lily in the meadow, the stag in the forest, the fish in the sea, and the joyful people sing: God is love! But under all the sopranos, as if it were a sustained bass part, sounds the de profundis of the sacrificed: God is Love![7]

Questions for reflection/discussion:
1. What does the apostle Paul mean by us being enemies with God? Cross-reference: Romans 5:8–10.
2. Name some changes that occur when a person surrenders his or her life to Christ?
3. In your own words, describe what total adherence to Christ as Lord means?
4. Why does sin block or hinder our fellowship with God?
5. According to Romans 10:9–10, what must we do to become a Christian?
6. What steps can I take to effect real, lasting change in my life?

Chapter 6: A Clean Heart

Be merciful to me according to Your great compassion…create in me a clean heart, O God, and renew a steadfast spirit within me.
—Psalms 51:1,10

A good way to begin our prayers is to humbly say, "God have mercy on me." God loves to extend mercy and grace to people whom society has written off. The world wrongly believes that failures, losers, and outcasts deserve no grace, no compassion, and no second chances. But the message of God in the Bible is so different. From the very beginning, there was a clear tension with God and man. Over and over in the Bible, we see that God was willing to do anything to save, help, and love humanity, but humanity is typically bent to do its own thing, and thus, dishonor and disobey God. Matthew explains that Jesus saw the multitudes as sheep without a shepherd and was filled with compassion.[1] That Greek phrase, "filled with compassion," means topped off—overflowing.

Jesus sympathizes with our weakness. He cares for us. "For we do not have a high priest who cannot sympathize with our weaknesses but one who has been tempted in all things as we are, yet without sin."[2] The word "sympathy" comes from two Greek words, *sym* and *pathos*, meaning to suffer with. Jesus suffered for us, but He also suffers with us. He understands. He knows our tears, hears our cries, and is patient with our questions.

One of the most astonishing stories of the Bible is found in the book of Hosea. Hosea was the prophet of Israel. He was God's anointed prophet for that time. He was God's man to lead and show God's people the message of God. At that time, Israel was chasing after other gods. To display a living example of His love and grace, God asked the prophet Hosea to marry a prostitute name Gomer. Gomer gives birth to three children with Hosea and then runs off to live with another man. She tricks on the streets, causing shame and embarrassment to her husband. Nothing is more humiliating to a man's pride than to live with an unhappy and unfaithful wife. Surely the town seethed in gossip and slander over this open scandal.

God told Hosea to love her and do whatever it took to win her back. He was to show himself as lovesick for Gomer.

Meanwhile, Gomer hit rock bottom. She ran up some debts and was sold into slavery on the public auction block for sale in the center of town. Hosea showed up to see his battered and broken wife standing in chains, naked and exposed, before the world. His heart broke, and he became the butt of lots of jokes and criticism as he purchased his wife back. She deserved death according to the Old Testament Law, but Hosea gave her unconditional love, grace, and mercy.

Addictions and Attitudes

In my prison cell, I do a lot of writing, reading, and praying. Everyday for about thirty to forty-five seconds, I hear the rhythmic pounding of a balled-up fist on the table into a heavy metal desktop. I know what is going on. I have had at least five different cellies who have practiced this daily ritual. A near by neighbor has just crushed up some pills and is preparing to viciously snort the powder with an explosive force of air through his nasal cavity. He then will hold his head back, tap the bridge of his nose, and with his eyes closed, he will violently shake his brain. Then, he uses toilet paper to wipe the blood running down his nose to his upper lip. After that he will be good for a couple of hours until he needs to repeat the process. In time, his supply and money will dry up, and his body will contract into what is called dope sickness. He is most dangerous when he reaches this stage. Being in close quarters in these situations causes great friction and can lead to violent episodes. There are numerous reported and unreported incidents in various prison cells that include murder. Familiarity breeds contempt, and there are few domestic disputes that compare to being confined and caged in a seven-by-twelve cell with another person that is troubled, addicted, and even psychotic.

    I flew on a Conair plane from Oklahoma City back to Atlanta and sat next to an inmate who had stabbed and killed his cellmate and then stabbed two prison guards in a melee back in the 1970s. The two guards had to be life-flighted to the hospital and barely lived. He was only nineteen but lost all control with his cellie over some prison drug deals and debts. He began prison with only two years to do, but he turned it into a life sentence in the Florida State pen. He spent the first nine years in the hole after getting all his teeth knocked out by the guards with a daily beating for the first four months of solitary. Thirty-five years later, he was paroled. He met a girl who visited him while he was in prison and got married. He was out of prison for ten years and happily married, working as a welder, but was caught with a gun in his house. His neighbor told on him. He picked up an ACCA (Armed Career Criminal Act) mandatory minimum sentence of fifteen more years at sixty-four years of age. He arrived at his new prison, got in a fight with his cellie, and stabbed him too, but he did not kill him. History repeated itself. Now, he was on the plane next to me being transferred to a higher security prison.

I flattered him by asking him how he got through nine years of solitary and kept his sanity. He said the only book he could have was a Bible, which he read nine times in nine years. He could write one letter per week, had no visits, no phone calls, and no commissary. I asked him if he believed in God. He said, "Off and on."

I then asked, "How did you do thirty-five years of time?"

He grinned from ear to ear and said, "I stayed high and drunk the entire time."

I said, "So, you never really got to know God?"

He held his head down when he said it, "No. Not really."

I really don't know why I asked the probing, yet personal, question, but I could not resist. "Have you ever apologized for what you did?"

In chains with a black box, anger and irritation filled his demeanor. He spit it as he said it, "Hell no. Why would I ever do that?"

His response burdened me. After a couple of moments of silence, I softly and gently pushed it out, "Because you can never be completely right with God or humankind if you do not acknowledge and repent of your sins."

We flew the rest of the flight in silence, and I watched him waddle away in a different direction as he went to his next prison location. I prayed for him, but I could not help but think of Psalms 34:16, "The face of the Lord is against evildoers."

What we all need more than a "pardon from prison" is the overwhelming sense that God accepts us, owns us, holds us, affirms us, and will never let us go. Because sin separates us from God and each other, we cannot walk in this confidence and peace until we are clean through the shed blood of Christ. Was he beyond the grace of God?

King David

In the Old Testament, King David had committed adultery and murder, and in fear, decided to conceal or cover it up. He fell into lust over a woman named Bathsheba and then used his power and authority to call her to himself. Her husband was a valiant soldier in King David's army and was away in battle. David then committed adultery with Bathsheba, and she became pregnant. David planned a scheme to get her husband Uriah to sleep with Bathsheba. He called Uriah back from battle and encouraged him to lie with his wife, but Uriah would not. King David then tried to get him drunk, but Uriah was a man of principle and would not sleep with his wife while his fellow soldiers were fighting on the battlefield. David then conspired to have Uriah killed by placing him on the frontline of the battle and then ordering other troupes to withdraw from him leaving him alone to die at the hands of the enemy. David had Uriah murdered. In our time, he would have got an LWOP, or life without parole sentence. For the next year, David hid his sin and tried to go on with life as if there was no consequence to his sins.

To conceal means to cover up. When Adam and Eve were caught eating the forbidden fruit in the Garden of Eden, the first thing they did was to run and hide, thus blocking communication with a holy God who cannot be in sin's presence. When Moses killed the Egyptian soldier, he immediately buried the body and ran. Human nature is to hide what we have done wrong. Yet, our secret sins are always known by God. What we hide on earth, God will eventually reveal. Someone has said that what is done in secret, God will shout from the rooftop.

Holiness

God's most prominent attribute is holiness. Holiness is used over six hundred times in the Bible to describe the attributes of God. God's holiness or perfection forces separation from sin. If prayer is talking with a holy God, then sin is the one thing that blocks or hinders that communication. When we conceal our sins, our prayers are hindered.

Proverbs 28:13, "He who covers his transgression will not prosper." Psalms 66:18, "If I cherish iniquity in my heart, the Lord will not hear me." The Shorter Catechism explains, "Prayer is the offering up of our desires unto God for the things agreeable to His will, in the name of Christ, with confession of our sins and thankful acknowledgement of His mercies."

In my prison, I work in the GED education department, and because I write a lot, I often use the copy machine and printer. Copies cost 15 cents per page, and we buy copy cards from the commissary for $7.50. All inmates complain about the cost, especially those like me who are working on pages and pages of legal work with very limited resources. In prison, we are surrounded by con artists, and as a result, one inmate figured out how to rip off copies from the machine without paying for the copies. It is a simple little furtive step that supervisors in the educational department have not figured out. I watch inmates steal hundreds of copies every day. I know how to do it as well.

As a Christian, I face a moral and ethical dilemma. The Federal Bureau of Prisons (BOP) extorts my family everyday by overcharging me for phone calls, e-mails, commissary, and copy machine use. Why don't I just get some "payback" and steal back from the BOP and taxpayer? It only seems fair, and besides, it is just a few dollars. I listen to other inmates who rationalize, rant, and justify their stealing by saying, "I steal from the Feds who are stealing from me and punishing my family financially." They go on, "When I get back on them, even a little, it makes me feel like I am beating their wicked system."

In 1989 at a Georgia church where I was a member, we had a three-week-long series of "revival" meetings. It was a time our congregation set aside to seek God and draw close to Him. During some services we had some time where participants of the revival would testify as to what God was doing in their life. Several people confessed some of their private sins to the public. One man had been working at the nuclear power plant, and over the years, he had been secretly stealing tools and time from his employer. He felt convicted by the Holy Spirit to return tools or reimburse his company for his theft.

One night our church worship leader stood up and in deep humility confessed that he had been using postage stamps from the church office without paying for them for years. Because his sin and stealing was against the congregation and God, he asked the entire congregation to forgive him. He also reimbursed the church for what he believed was an accurate amount of what he had taken. It took a lot of courage for him to admit and confess this in front of the very people he was called to serve, but it was worth it to him to have a clear conscience before God and his fellow man. It made an impression on me, and as I served in various churches and in corporate America, I never wanted to steal or use anything that was not mine without permission or without properly paying for it.

    I could easily steal copies from the BOP and the American taxpayer, and no one would see me do it. Even other inmates would not know that I am stealing copies. I feel strongly that I have been oversentenced far beyond the true nature of my crimes. I feel most prisoners are way oversentenced, and the system is severely flawed—overwhelmingly stacked against the poor, uneducated, and oppressed. I have good reason to get some "vengeance." I hear some of my friends say they steal from the kitchen, do drugs, take paper, copies, disobey rules for only one reason: "to get some payback." They say, "I hate the police and anyone who associates with them."

    Here is the problem. God says in Exodus 20:15, "You shall not steal." God knows. God sees. And that is all that matters. He knows that stealing causes our lives to get out of sync or balance with Him. He knows it is a form of cheating. Stealing shows that I am not trusting God. He rewards obedience, and any disobedience in my life only brings conflict and punishment and impedes my relationship with God. I cannot hide or conceal my sin from God even if I fool the entire world.

Sin Begins in Our Thoughts

    David's sin began in his thoughts. He let his lust grow until it consumed him. He did not resist, turn away, or flee from the temptation. Because he did not repent immediately, but instead covered his sin, it spiraled out of control on him. One sin led to another and then another and then yet another. The consequences mounted against him. Eventually the prophet Nathan confronted David, and he immediately fell on his face and began the process of repenting, confessing, and forsaking his sin.

David's prayer of repentance in Psalm 51 expresses the heartfelt desire of David to be clean of sin and reconnected to his God. He humbly cried for God's mercy and forgiveness. We must do the same. God wants us to have a clean heart.

> The desired end of man is not happiness, nor health, but holiness. Gods one aim is the production of saints. (Oswald Chambers)[3]

Questions for reflection/discussion:
1. What happens when we choose to hide or cover our sins?
2. Name some consequences David experienced as a result of hiding his sin. Cross-reference: Psalms 32 and 38.
3. Privately list some or all sins in your life that have not been confessed or brought before God in repentance.
4. Why is it important to resolve all conflicts with other people and God?
5. Define holiness. Why does God want us to be holy? Cross-reference: 1 Peter 1:16; Hebrews 12:14.
6. Explain why it is important to confess our sins to God and others. Cross-reference: James 5:16; 1 John 1:9.

Action step: Join a friend for a time of prayer and confession of your sins (James 5:16). Ask God to heal the hurts of your heart and the sorrows of your past.

Chapter 7: Forgiveness

Blessed is he whose transgression is forgiven, whose sin is covered.
—Psalms 32:1

Making peace with our past sins and failures is not easy. My friend Sammy has a white mother and black father, and he tells me that all his life he was rejected by both races. He has no idea who or where his father is or if he is alive, even though he always longed to know his father. He has been a fatherless child since the day he was born.

Every child longs to be loved and known by his or her father. Any rejection or abandonment causes serious problems such as various inferiority complexes. As he told his story, honesty was in his sad eyes. I heard the pain in his voice, and I was reminded of *Homer's Odyssey*. It is a twenty-five-hundred-year-old Greek literature poem that tells the story of Telemachus, who leaves home on a dangerous journey in search of his missing father, Odysseus.[1] It is considered classic literature as it has been read and published almost as long as King David's prayers in the book of Psalms. The story of Odysseus moves me because it reveals that, even twenty-five hundred years ago, there were popular stories about a kid looking for his dad.

The truth is that we are all on a lifelong search for our father. We want our Heavenly Father, Creator, Purpose Giver first and our earthly father second. Understandably, a lot of fathers have such deep psychological and emotional problems that so consume their visual field that they have trouble seeing anyone but themselves, much less a lost and confused father-hungry kid. Thankfully, our Heavenly Father willingly and passionately adopted us and brought us into His eternal family of love and acceptance. Our spiritual family is more important than an earthly family because, for most of us, our earthly families are always being shattered by divorce, death, and abandonment.

I Want to See My Daddy

Not long ago I sat in the visitation room of prison basking in a state of pure bliss talking with my family. Directly across from us was another inmate with two small children and his girlfriend. His children's eyes told everyone in the room how much they adored their dad who was incarcerated. Their giant smiles bulged during those happy moments with their absentee dad as they ate candy and drank a soda. Dad held his young son on his lap, who was in big-boy Pull-Ups under his jeans. Then I saw him do it. I wasn't shocked in any kind of way because I've seen it often. It is the main reason prison visitation policies are so frustratingly restrictive and uncomfortable.

    The daddy quickly reached into his son's Pull-Ups, and with the sleight of hand, he furtively brought out a bag of dope and slid it into his own private area. Within the next minute, some officers came in and escorted him out. The cameras in prison are accurate, and as a result, the inmate did not come back. If he would have been successful, he could have sold the few grams of meth, coke, heroin, or whatever he had, for hundreds of dollars. The officers then came and took the woman and children out. The woman friend tried to play ignorant, but she will likely face a new charge of bringing contraband into a federal prison. The two small kids walked out with their faces altered in confusion. I heard one child somberly say, "But I want to see my daddy." Sadly, they won't see their daddy again for a long time. He will be put on visitation restriction among other disciplinary actions and may even face a new charge.

    Boys and girls need to be able to look into their father's eyes and see admiration and delight. No one wants their father's love for them to be a secret, and no child wants to be used to commit an illegal act. They want to be loved and adored by their dad. As fathers, we have the responsibility to give our kids comfort, confidence, courage, and practical help. For example, like being able to read a map or teach them how to love their enemies and where to find heart when adversity demands it of us, because life is much harder than we think we can endure. Abandoning our kids causes irreversible damage.

Sammy

My friend Sammy spent most of his life in the ghetto, in and out of group homes, foster homes, and living with various unattached relatives. Sexually molested as a child, he has spent his entire life looking for his father, and when he did not find him, anger and vengeance against his world took over. His criminal record began building during his early teenage years. It was filled with everything from petty theft to violent acts of assault. His mother was around only part of the time, and with little guidance, discipline, or direction, he quit school like so many of his friends. Juvenile detention was just part of the course. He experienced life in big blasts—hip-hop style; he only understood the viscous side of life.

    At age fifteen he was arrested for grand theft auto. When he was sixteen, his grandfather, the only man in his life, died, and this loss broke his heart. The very next morning, he found his mother dead of a morphine overdose from her father's leftover medicine. It was a double blow. Sammy continued to run the streets with various gangs. He fathered five children with four different women who were all jealous for his attention. The easy money from drugs and thievery filled the temporary highs of pleasure and ego. No one ever took time to teach him responsibility, discipline, or model parenthood. At age twenty-two, he hit some dead end streets. Desperate and in need of quick cash, he carjacked a man and demanded his ride and money at gunpoint. He got away with it and decided to try it again. This time he was caught. The Feds picked up the charge, and because of his past, he was labeled an armed career criminal. He faced life in prison, and sadly, all life sentences in the Feds have no parole, even those with no murder, no child molestation, terrorism, or actual violence. Parole was sadly eliminated in the Feds in 1986. For people serving LWOP, the only hope of freedom is some type of law change, presidential pardon, or clemency. The depression is deep for these individuals because there is no incentive to change, program, heal, or live with any real hope. In the land of the free and home of the brave, it is hard to believe that LWOPs are fairly common even for relatively nonviolent offenders who are abandoned, forgotten, and left to rot away in prison.

    While in the county jail, Sammy connected quickly with other criminals joining in their violent talk, aggressive behavior, and pursuit of any kind of high they could find. After three months of the rising stress and the hideous grind of daily confinement in the county jail, he got his hands on a Bible and started reading. He told me, "I don't know why, but I could not put it down. I read and read and read. I even missed a lot of meals because I did not want to quit reading." Not long after that, he prayed to receive Christ into his life, and he meant it with all of his heart. It was not just jailhouse religion, nor a passing fad to garner sympathy from his court or victims. For the next ten months, he attended church in jail every chance he could and stayed faithful to his commitment to Christ. When sentencing came, he was given 447 months or a little over 37 years in federal prison. At age twenty-two, without any law changes or some kind of miracle release, if he survives, he will not see freedom again until he is in his mid-fifties, no matter how much he improves, programs, and keeps good behavior. Most who do this type of time become severely institutionalized.

When I met him, he had completed almost eleven years of his sentence. In my three years of prison, I have yet to meet another Christian who has such great faith. This guy loves God with a deep and dedicated commitment. His positive attitude, high-energy thinking, and enthusiasm for God are simply inspirational. In fact, I would be hard-pressed to find another committed Christian in thirty-four years of active Christian church experience who gives himself to prayer and the work of Christ like Sammy does now. He spends every day in prayer and worship, setting aside certain days to fast and pray. He leads multiple Bible studies every day of the week and witnesses for Christ in a very difficult prison. Many people have come to Christ because of his witness.

He exudes the spirit of Christ's love in everything he does and says. Honesty is in his humble-looking eyes, but high hopes and faith-based thinking rule his heart. Since being in prison, Sammy has completed his GED, and he has also completed an associates degree with plans to complete his bachelor's degree very soon. He has had no disciplinary shots, no drugs, and has kept model behavior.

Meeting people like Sammy always causes me to be spellbound by their stories—none quite like Sammy, mainly because of his devoted faith. After twenty-three years of growing up in hell and making a terrible mess of his life, he has now logged eleven years of faithfulness. (Someone please let him go! How much punishment is enough?)

I asked Sammy about his case and his two carjacked victims and how he resolved his offenses toward them. He told me that after he became a Christian, God led him to make a statement of apology before the court. His victims and their families were present. At his sentencing hearing, he explained, "I know I did wrong, and I am very sorry. I hope that one day you can find it in your heart to forgive me." He was given an order by the court to not attempt to contact his victims, and so far, neither victim has responded to his apologies. It burdens him, but he did all he could do to make things right within the court order.

Sammy shows grace to all offenders. He likes to say, "Hurt people often hurt people." Everyone is either the one dishing out the hurt or being hurt. It is part of the imperfect world of humanity. He believes that is why Jesus stressed loving our enemies, doing good to those who hurt us, praying for those we dislike, and forgiving even our worst enemies. When we return love for hate, we express the peace of God within us.

Forgiveness and Trust

Sammy's victims do not have to trust him, but they do have an obligation to forgive him. There is a difference between trust and forgiveness. Forgiveness means to let go of the past or to release the offender. Trust has to do with future behavior. Jesus has taught that all relationships are worth restoring, and forgiveness is where the healing begins. Sammy has now rebuilt relationships with all his children, ex-girlfriends, and extended family. He has also added many new Christian friends from all over the world. Love and peace crown his life.

I asked Sammy to tell me how he would teach others the steps to rebuild a broken relationship. Here is what he said:

1. *Pray first and give it to God.* Pray continually for those you have offended or who have offended you. Jesus said, "Pray for your enemies. Bless those who curse you. Do good to those who hurt you." [2]

2. *In a spirit of prayer and genuine humility, take the initiative.* Do what you can to reach out to the offended party. When Adam and Eve sinned against God, they went and hid. God sought them in the garden. God took the initiative to make things right even though God was the one offended. When humanity sinned against God, we all became enemies of God.[3] He is just, and we are unjust.

This tension creates hostility, anger, and fear between God and us. But God took the initiative and sent Jesus to bridge the gap or restore the broken relationship. When relationships are broken between a father and son, or mother and daughter, or neighbors, or church members, or whomever, we are instructed to take the initiative to try and repair the problem.[4] Jesus instructed us that, before we pray, leave our gift and go make things right with our brother and then come back and pray or connect with God the Father.

3. *Confess your part of the conflict and take responsibility for your part.* Acknowledge your own errors and "man up" for your wrongs.

4. *Don't just say, "I am sorry."* Express "I am sorry. I was wrong. Will you forgive me?" Now, the responsibility is in their hands.

5. *If restitution is necessary, do what you can to repay or meet the restitution requirements.*

Clearing our conscience with people we have offended requires that we do our part. We take time to express our apology and do everything we can to make things right. After that, it is in God's hands. When, not "if," we are wronged, we must be prepared to forgive our offenders in advance. If we do not, our prayers will be hindered.

I remember driving around the traffic mess of Atlanta, Georgia, in the middle of my busy investment business days. Over the course of years, I would get stuck on Georgia 400 or I-285, and there were so many times when people in a hurry would cut me off. I had to think in advance to reject low-energy thinking of anger and bitterness and go ahead and wave my hand in a friendly manner, letting them know they are forgiven—"no big deal." The world we live in demands that we are prepared to forgive and release others who both intentionally and unintentionally are going to hurt, harm, or offend us. However, it is in forgiving others that we learn and experience forgiveness ourselves. In 1 Corinthians 13, the apostle Paul said, "love endures all things."

Why should we live in a spirit of love, grace, and forgiveness? Simple. We want our prayers answered and our fellowship with God vibrant and alive. Something in our past may be impeding God's flow to the present. Resentment blocks our relationship with Him. If we do not forgive those who sin against us, our Heavenly Father will not forgive us.[5] When we refuse to do good to others while we have the power and opportunity to do so, the blessing of God is restricted on our lives.

Forgiving Much, Loves Much

Jesus was having dinner with Simon the Pharisee when a woman of ill repute came in, bowed at His feet, and began weeping and washing His feet with the tears from her face.[6] She wanted to be near Jesus. Simon showed no grace and was indignant toward her. He viewed her as a sad and sick pariah. But Jesus always lifted up the long shot. He viewed people differently by always seeing their potential. Why did she show such affection to Jesus? Because she was forgiven much. Jesus made the point that he who is forgiven much, loves much. Here is a difficult truth for all of us to grasp: *We will never be asked by God to forgive anyone, anything more than we have already been forgiven.* When we return love and forgiveness for hate, we express the peace of God that lives within us. I finish this chapter with one of my favorite prayers to contemplate:

> Where there is hatred, let me sow love;
> Where there is injury, pardon;
> Where there is doubt, faith;
> Where there is despair, light;
> Where there is sadness, joy;
> O divine Master, grant that I may not so much seek
> to be consoled as to console;
> To be understood as to understand,
> To be loved as to love;
> For it is in giving that we receive;
> It is in pardoning that we are pardoned;
> It is in dying to self that we are born to eternal life.
> (St. Francis of Assisi)[7]

Questions for reflection/discussion:
1. Describe what it feels like to be condemned? What would it feel like to be pardoned?
2. Why is our spiritual family more important than our earthly family?
3. How do we express the peace and grace of God that lives within us?
4. What happens to our communication with God when we refuse to forgive? Cross-reference: Matthew 6:14–15.
5. List the benefits of having a clear conscience. Cross-reference: 1 Timothy 1:5–6.
6. Why is God's forgiveness dependent upon our willingness and commitment to forgive those who offend us?

Chapter 8: The Poison That Kills

Have mercy on us, Oh Lord, have mercy on us. For we are exceedingly filled with contempt.
—Psalms 123:3

I watched and listened as Tool, an out-of-control, malice-filled, offended inmate lost his temper and violently attacked a friend of mine named Memphis. Memphis, an addict himself, owed him some drugs that Tool had given him to hold for him. Tool did not want to be caught with the drugs so he asked Memphis to hold them for him until later. To reward Memphis, Tool told him he could have a small piece of the dope. When it came time for Tool to retrieve his drugs, Memphis had snorted all of it for himself, and Tool was livid. There is a saying among drug dealers and users that goes like this: "Monkeys can not sell bananas, and addicts can not hold other people's dope."

In the big picture, the offense was over a rather small amount of contraband worth about forty dollars. Compared to Tool's crimes on the street of at least three attempted murders, and more attempts of which he was not charged, I stressed that I thought he could show a little grace to my friend Memphis. I even told him I would pay for the loss if he would just let it go. In addition, Tool was known on the compound for running up drug debts and then not paying them. Eventually, like many other prison-compound addicts, Tool will run up a large debt with the wrong people and then secretly check in to protective custody with some lame excuse.

With eyes of fire, the dope sick Tool yelled, "I will never forgive him or trust him again. He is not my friend, nor will he ever be. When I get a chance, I am going to **** up his ****. I hate that **********!" I did not doubt him in the least. His anger was frightening, and for someone who had already done over half his life in prison, additional punishment in the way of more time was not a deterrent. In a fit of rage and fury, Tool impulsively beat Memphis in a vicious and barbaric manner. Memphis was hurt and did not come out of his cell for the next three days.

Another friend told me about a similar situation in one of his past prisons. A man was about to be released to go home in twelve days after serving almost ten years, but he had a conflict with another inmate who owed him thirty-six dollars over some drugs. They got into a violent confrontation, and the man about to be released killed the other inmate. He stabbed him in the heart with a shank. The tragic event happened right in front him. That man went from going home in twelve days to a new life sentence and a lot of time in ADX (supermax). The other man's life came to a sudden and violent end.

A couple of days later, I sat down with Tool. Tool claimed to be a Christian who had a jailhouse conversion years ago. He even loved old-time gospel singing; however, he was neither remorseful nor repentant but was proud of his stand. Our conversation culminated with, "Anyone who claims to be a Christian must live in love toward other people. We have been forgiven much by Christ. We also have an obligation to forgive much. We cannot say we hate others and have love in our heart for God."

He looked at me and said, "Price, that might work for you in the free world, but it will not work here in prison. The code requires a beat down, and that is what Memphis got. You have a lot of learning to do." Insolent, he said, "I am an OG before I am a Christian. I always will be." OG stands for "original gangster." He then stormed away.

I thought about Tool and how he compensates for his absence of self-worth by acting as if he has an overabundance of it. He is grandiose. He expects to be treated as superior to other people, acts entitled, can't admit wrong, and will never apologize because he is never to blame for anything. His hunger for admiration and attention is insatiable. He cannot give importance to other people's emotions, feelings, or failures, and he is incapable of empathy. He can't love—not even his own children or family. At first blush, he is charming and seems competent and confident. He is a natural entertainer, at times funny, outgoing, and even flattering to some people. But inside he is empty, self-loathing, and much more fragile than he lets on. It is all part of his ever-growing ego and the constant feeding of his resentment.

Resentment

Resentment breeds contempt. In three years of jail and prison, I have listened to hundreds, maybe even thousands, of conversations from other inmates who speak of the revenge they will get one day. "Get backs" will be sweet, and unfortunately, that becomes the driving force of daily "very low energy" thoughts. Booker T. Washington said, "I shall let no man belittle my soul by making me hate him!"[1]

Nothing blocks our relationship with God like bitterness and unforgiveness. Hebrews 12:15 warns, "Do not resist the grace of God lest a root of bitterness springs up in you like Esau, a godless man." Bitterness is resentment toward God. It is contempt for God's plan and how He is working in our life. It means we do not believe that God has our good in mind in all things.

Instant confession of sin and the receiving of God's forgiveness are inexplicably linked to our own forgiveness and mental health. It is impossible to have a right relationship with God when we are bitter and resentful toward other people. According to 1 John 4:7–8, "He that loves not, knows not God, for God is love." Bitterness is just like rat-poison pellets. They only have a small amount of poison in the pellet, but it only takes a small amount to kill.

Everyone of us has been done wrong many times. Offenses build up. From the very beginning of time, history is replete with examples of one nation attacking another nation over offenses that occur generations before. Think of Genghis Khan, arguably one of the greatest military strategists of all time. For hundreds of years, the Chin people attacked and raided the unorganized and fragmented Mongolian tribes. Genghis united his people and finally led them to fight back to protect their lands, women, and children. After some convincing victories, he raided the Chin people and conquered their land. The pride and ego that consumed him led him to a bloodlust desire to conquer many other nations, which included the killing and raping of millions of people. His conquest began with revenge, and his life ended by revenge. Jesus said, "[F]or all who live by the sword will perish by the sword."[2]

Why did Jesus say that you love your enemies, do good to those who persecute you, and pray for those who intentionally hurt you? Because the poison of resentment can easily take over. Almost everyone in prison feels betrayed by his or her government and society. We feel like we have got a bad deal and been punished way beyond the true nature of our crimes. This attitude can quickly turn into bitterness and resentment, which will spill over into every relationship. Bitterness is a poison that must be eliminated. It blocks our communion and peace with God.

I often get questions about vengeance and justice. Vengeance is not ours to take. It is God's. We trust God to work out all things for us. He has perfect judgment and settles all accounts and debts in His own time and way. Take time to read Romans 12:17–13:2. Vengeance is for God alone. We are assigned no part of it.

Legend of Moses

The legend of Moses is a tale that was made up to help illustrate how God takes care of justice and vengeance. A legend says that Moses once sat near a well in meditation. A traveler stopped to drink from the well, and when he did so, his purse accidently fell from his belt and into the sand. The man departed and did not notice his purse was left behind. Shortly afterward, another man passed near the well, saw the purse, and picked it up and left. Later, a third man stopped at the wall to assuage his thirst and went to sleep in the shadow of the well.

Meanwhile, the first man noticed his purse was missing. Assuming he must have lost it at the well, he returned and woke up the sleeper who of course knew nothing of the purse. The first man demanded his money back. An argument followed, and irate, the first man slew the latter. Where upon Moses said to God, "You see, that is why men do not believe in You. There is too much evil and injustice in the world. Why should the first man have lost his purse and then become a murderer? Why should the second have got a purse full of gold without having worked for it? The third was completely innocent. Why was he slain?

God answered, "For once and only once, I will give you an explanation. I cannot do it at every step of life. The first man was a thief's son. The purse contained money stolen by his father from the father of the second man, who finding the purse only found what was due to him. The third was a murderer whose crime had never been revealed and who received from the first man the punishment he deserved." In the future, believe there is a sense of righteousness in what transpires even when you don't understand.[3]

There are many illustrations throughout history that express this same idea. One of my favorites is the story of the notorious Roman general and consul of Rome, Julius Gaius Caesar. In 44 BC,

Caesar was murdered by his childhood best friend and lifelong protector, Brutus. We get the word "brutality" from the man named Brutus. Caesar was stabbed twenty-three times by other senators of Rome, and Brutus himself led the effort. Each stabbed the hero of Rome once. They did not want him to become emperor. What is interesting is that Roman history explains that every single man who had a hand in Caesar's murder died a gruesome death. Each lived in fear and peril up to the point of their deaths. Even Brutus was surrounded by Mark Anthony and Octavian's (adopted nephew of Caesar and eventual emperor of Rome—Caesar Augustus, August for "awe inspiring one worthy of worship," who ruled the Roman Empire when Christ was born in 4 BC) forces before taking his own life in utter defeat and humiliation. Not one of Caesar's murderers died in the comfort of their bed at a ripe old age with a clear conscience.

    God knows the intricate details of our lives. He knows our case history and the efforts we have made to make things right and turn our lives around. He knows how hard we work to change, heal, and become a better person. Justice and vengeance are God's, and God always renders perfect justice that is balanced and overwhelmingly full of grace. If we all got what we deserved, we would be given eternal punishment in hell. Let God handle the vengeance. His judgment is perfect. Ours is always flawed. Our mandate is to love, and we cannot love others when we are judging them.

Poison

According to Hebrews, bitterness is a deadly poison that once it enters the soul, it destroys all joy. Esau is described as a godless and immoral person because of his resentment. Resentful people have no faith in God's perfect plan. Because they do not understand grace and forgiveness (do not resist the grace of God), they do not know how to forgive and show grace to others. Bitterness is also a major factor leading to sexual immorality. Esau was described as an immoral person because of his bitterness toward God and others.

    Think once again of the woman of ill repute named Mary who understood she was forgiven much, and as a result, she loved much.[4] One thing we can all do, and strive to do with extreme abandon, is love God. This woman loved Jesus much because she realized how much and how many sins she had been forgiven. She bowed before him in passionate worship and adored Him. People who understand how much they have been forgiven have no problem forgiving others.

Bitterness is one of the three main root sins we find in the Bible: greed, pride, and bitterness. If we are going to change, survive, and thrive in prison, we must conquer all three sins. We are either going to get better or grow bitter. I do not have to remind you that we are in jail or prison and around people who have been through the incarceration process over and over again. The wear, tear, and stress of resentment show on everyone's face. Living in forgiveness and grace toward angry, selfish, and hateful people is a test of our maturity and trust in Christ. In fact, every temptation and trial are like a job interview. God is watching how we handle things.

How Many Times?

Peter asked Jesus how many times we should forgive, seven times?[5] Using hyperbole (an expression of exaggeration), Jesus told him 77 times or 70 × 7 times. We are not to keep count and forgive 490 trespasses. Jesus meant unlimited times. We are to forgive others just as our Father in heaven has forgiven us.[6]

Jesus told the parable of a master who wished to settle an insurmountable debt with one of his slaves who did not have the ability to repay his debt.[7] Keep in mind that, in ancient culture, slaves made up about 50 percent of the population. You were either a slave or free. Jesus described the debt as an astronomical amount of money that the slave owed. He could not pay it back in one hundred lifetimes. The master decided to sell the slave and his family into slavery where, under Jewish Law, they would be forced to work for six full years and then be set free on the seventh year. The slave fell to his master's feet and begged for mercy. The master felt compassion, and in amazing grace, decided to release the debt and fully forgive the slave.

The forgiven slave went out and found one of his fellow slaves who owed him a very small amount of money. The forgiven slave demanded the money immediately, and his fellow slave fell to the ground and begged for mercy as well. He said, "Have patience with me, and I will repay you." The forgiven slave was unwilling to release the debt, and he had his fellow slave bound and thrown into debtor's prison.

The forgiven slave's master heard of what he had done and summoned him. He said, "You *wicked* slave, I forgave you all the debt you owned because you pleaded with me. Should you have not have had mercy on your fellow slave in the same way that I had mercy on you" (emphasis added)? In anger the master handed him over to the torturers until he should repay what was owed him.

Jesus finished the story by saying, "My heavenly Father will also do the same to you, if each of you does not forgive his brother from your heart."[8] Jesus's teaching on forgiveness toward others is unconditional. Forgiveness is unearned and undeserved. There is no "but he or she did." Jesus said to release the offense. Forgive. Move on. He does not say we have to trust the offender, but he does say we have to forgive—and live in mercy and grace toward others. God warns that judgment will be merciless to the one who has shown no mercy (James 2:13).

Something Terrible in Us

I have attended two thirteen-week drug rehab programs in prison. One of them was a weekly AA/NA (Alcoholics Anonymous/Narcotics Anonymous) program. I had to humbly introduce myself each week with "Hello. My name is Lee Price. I am an addict." I have never been a drug addict or an alcoholic. I have been addicted to work. I have been addicted to financial markets. I have been addicted to making money. I have been addicted to sinful pleasures. I have been addicted to my own self-righteousness. The truth is, I will always be susceptible to sin, so I am not ashamed to publicly proclaim my own sinfulness.

At one of my meetings, an older black man who had done years and years of time broke down in tears in front of twenty other hardened inmates. He said, "I have to confess that I have something horrible in me. It is called hate. I hate my country. I hate my government. I hate that I hate the very people I am supposed to love." He continued, "I am a drug addict. I can't stop. But I do not know what to do. I do not know how to overcome. This hate I feel is what is driving me to desire the escape I get from drugs." I spoke to

Kenneth later and broke down the idea of bitterness and the alternative of "release," because bitterness is a root sin. Many other sins spring from the root of bitterness. By forgiving others I am trusting that God is better at justice than I am. God is much better than me to balance justice and mercy. In fact, I do not need to judge. Jesus said, "Judge not lest you be judged. For with what measure you use to judge, the same measure will be used against you." (Matt. 7:1)

Extreme Forgiveness

Forgiveness from God is no good if we cannot forgive others. Grace and forgiveness signify giving people what they do not deserve, but it is for our own good. Bitterness and vengeance are easy, but the love of God through us is supreme.[9] Love bears or endures all things. Christ showed us how to treat others with grace. He walked away from hostility. He loved the unloved. He forgives our wickedness. Paul says in Ephesians 4:32, "Be kind to one another, tender hearted, forgiving each other, just as God in Christ Jesus has forgiven you." Remember that God will never ask us to forgive someone more than He has already forgiven us. The true test of Christianity is love, and we only love God as much as the person we hate the most.

I recently read a story of extreme forgiveness. A German missionary and his family moved to Malatya, Turkey, to share the gospel of Christ with a Muslim community. One Sunday, the husband and father of three children led an Easter service where three Muslims faked interest in Christianity. After the service they scheduled an appointment with the pastor and two of his assistants to learn more about Christianity. Each radical Muslim arrived with a bag of makeshift torture devices under their arm. They locked the door and then took their time taking apart the "infidels" for their heresy, piece by piece. Afterward the German widow was put under tremendous pressure to leave the mission field. The widow told the local Turkish paper, "We have been in Malatya for over ten years now. Everyone respected and cared for us. I want to forgive my husband's assassins because I believe they don't know what they have done. My husband was killed in the name of Jesus Christ, and because of his love for Him. We want to go on living here. My children go to school here, and I want my husband to be buried in the city cemetery so my son can go and place flowers on his grave and in so doing, draw strength to go on hoping and believing."[10]

Loving our enemies may be the hardest thing in the world to do. We cannot do it apart from God's grace. Forgiveness is unearned. It is total grace. At every place I have had to do time, there are always multiple inmates who are a thorn in everyone's side. They are dirty, mean, angry, and selfish. Also, there has always been at least one correctional officer who lives in a spirit of revenge and hostility. They think of us as animals in a cage to be poked and harassed. All these people are great opportunities to practice grace and forgiveness.

The world that we live in fosters a spirit of anger and resentment. Bitterness is a strong temptation, but love is supreme. We must not fall into the lowest level of "bitter thinking" that leads to all kinds of other sins and conflicts. God forgave us our sins, so let us be quick to forgive and release others of their sins against us. We are never more like God than when we are forgiving our enemies and loving those who hurt us. God's peace and love will flow naturally through our lives. We will abide in Him, and He in us, and that connection is the highest level of human thinking. It is ultimate Christianity. It is ultimate life.

John 3:16: "For God so loved the world that He gave His only begotten Son that whosoever believes in Him should not perish but have eternal life." God so loved that He gave. He *for*gave. Jesus cried from the cross, "Father forgive them, for they know not what they are doing."[11]

Verse to memorize:

> When a man's ways please the Lord, he makes even his enemies to be at peace with him. (Prov. 16:7)

Meditate: Live a life of no excuses but to trust God in continual prayer. According to the Bible, everything I want, desire, and need is already here. I have just not fully connected to Christ yet. But when I do, I shall never see myself as lacking in strength again. What others think of me is none of my business. My strength is in connecting to God alone, and that strength does not know weakness.

Questions for reflection/discussion:
1. Define forgiveness, bitterness, and grace.
2. Why should we pray or appeal to Gods mercy for our lives?
3. What is the main reason that the woman of ill repute in Luke 7 fell before Christ in such humility and brokenness?
4. List the reasons why bitterness is the result of resisting God's grace.
5. Name (to yourself) the people whom you know you need to pray for and forgive.
6. What action step or act of kindness can you take to smash the bitterness you feel for certain people?
7. Why is it important to bless those who curse you, do good to those who hurt you, and pray for your enemies?

Chapter 9: Forbidden Desires

Lord make me chaste, just not yet.
—St. Augustine

The ancient Greeks used the word *epithumia* to describe earnest desire or impulsive lust. It is an intense longing, especially for that which is forbidden. In the New Testament, *epithumia* is used thirty-one times to describe "lust or evil desire for a forbidden thing." The notable philosopher Aristotle used *epithumia* to describe a groping or unlawful pleasure. The Stoics defined *epithumia* as a desire after forbidden delight that defied all reason. Most people are in prison because they did things that defiled "all reason." The apostle James described *epithumia*, or sinful desire, as something that has conceived, gives birth to sin, and when it is full grown, it brings forth death.[1]

John Piper says, "Sin is what you do when your heart is not satisfied with God. We sin because it holds out some promise of happiness. That sin enslaves us until we believe that God is more to be desired than anything else in life. Sin's promises are broken by God's promises. Sin is a fleeting pleasure." The apostle Peter tells us that we are to be holy because He is holy, and the writer of Hebrews says that without holiness no one will see the Lord.[2] Thankfully, Jesus is our holiness.

Recently I was placed in the SHU (special housing unit). The SHU is also known as the hole, and sometimes you are stuck in a cell with another inmate for twenty-four hours a day. It is unpleasant in every imaginable way. I was moved into a cell with another inmate whom I had never seen or met. I immediately noticed he was reading a stack of erotica romance novels, and of course, it was like an alarm went off in my spirit that I was possibly celling with a sex offender. He promised me he was not a sex offender and explained he had a drug charge. I try not to judge certain offenses more harshly than others, but there are some sex crimes that cause discomfort only because of other very inappropriate and even despicable encounters I have faced in various jails.

Sure enough, he had a sex charge and not a drug charge. He told me he had read over seven hundred erotic novels since being in prison. Every thought and conversation he had returned to sexual activity. He was consumed by lust. I was soon moved out of the cell, but not before I learned his story. He had repeatedly raped and molested his own six-year-old daughter and eight-year-old son, videotaped the encounters, and then distributed it over the Internet. His court had no mercy on him and gave him twenty-five years.

As I have listened to and documented many conversations with various sex offenders, the stories are all similar. As a child they were molested or raped by a parent, sibling, stepparent, stepbrother, cousin, neighbor, teacher, or priest. One man I met in Jacksonville, Florida, at the Baker County Fed holdover, had just received a life sentence for molesting his stepchildren. It was his third serious offense. He seemed very broken and repentant, but three times? Does he deserve any compassion? Can he be healed, delivered, and saved by Christ, or is he and others like him condemned to an eternal hell because Jesus said it would be better to hang a millstone around his neck and be thrown to the bottom of the sea if you harm one of these?[3] Is he and so many others like him beyond God's grace? The biblical answer is absolutely not. No one is beyond God's grace, and no matter what our charges, we all can praise God for this truth. There is a sin unto death,[4] so if you are still alive, God has given you grace and the opportunity to repent and beg for mercy. No one is ever beyond God's grace.

Moral Purity

Long and often, as a young Christian, I mulled over the idea of moral purity and what to do with the demands of the flesh. I had ambivalence toward certain ideas. On the one hand, I desired chastity to give my heart completely to God's perfect will. On the other hand, our culture is consumed with the lust of the flesh. In prison we have an opportunity to purify and perfect our thoughts from lust. The availability of pornography is somewhat limited with no Internet access, and if one stays accountable, it is possible to do all your time and not have to look at a single picture of porn. By God's grace I seek to spend all my prison years intentionally avoiding all immoral activity including romance novels full of erotic stories and the circulation of various types of pornography. Self-control is a fruit of the Spirit of God living in us. Dr. Scott Peck explains self-control as delayed gratification. He says, "Delayed gratification is a process of scheduling the pain and pleasure of life in such a way as to enhance the pleasure by meeting and experiencing the pain first and getting it over with. It is the only decent way to live."[5]

While I was in the Bulloch County Jail, I was forced to cell for one night with a child rapist who was back on a parole violation. Sadly, the man was sadistically consumed with homosexual passions while in prison, and he was possessed with his past pedophile activities and his victims. He had tattooed all kinds of naked pictures on all parts of his body including his privates, and he arrogantly told stories and jokes of the children he had raped and fantasized to rape. He paraded his crime as something noble or cute. We know that God says we should never boast in evil.[6] My behavior was far from restrained when I physically confronted the rapist that same day and then was moved to another cell. Sinful desires are like a gigantic, selfish monster who never wants to let us go. This monster is the source of all impulsive and irrational behavior.

God Turns Us Over to Our Wicked Passions

When a person chooses lawlessness, impulsive *epithumia*, giving into the forbidden, perverted, and wicked pleasures, he ceases to be aware of God and that which is right and wrong. His conscience is seared, possibly beyond repair. Romans tell us that God turns certain individuals over to their degrading and depraved passions.[7] *Epithumia* represents the perverted, unreasonable desire for some forbidden object. Lustful desire can exert so much power over a person's mind that they do outrageous and shameful things. The end of *epithumia*, according to the scriptures, is death. As John Piper likes to say, we must be killing lust, or it will kill us. Paul says, "For this is the will of God, your sanctification; that is, that you abstain from sexual immorality; that each of you possess his own vessel in sanctification and honor, not in lustful passion."[8] Then Paul exhorts, "Flee youthful lusts and pursue righteousness, faith, love and peace with those who call on the Lord with a pure heart."[9]

One of my many cellies was renting out his porno magazines to child molesters and sex offenders. It made me so angry that I called him out on it and changed cells. It was a righteous anger, and I am glad I stood against him and other sex offenders who involved themselves in this sin. At the same time, I believe God is pleased with those with sex crimes who have genuinely repented, show remorse, and are putting forth great effort to get better. Regardless of our crimes, we all need grace, and we all should be begging God for mercy before the great day of wrath. God's mercy is our only hope.

Lust

All lust begins in our thoughts. David saw Bathsheba, lusted over her beauty, and consciously made a decision that he wanted her. His thinking became foggy and flawed because of covetousness and forbidden desire. It led to disorganized and irrational thoughts. Sometimes our troubles occur because we are just plain ignorant or impaired. We lose simple common sense. Stupid is repeating the same things over and over and expecting a different result. We cannot fill our minds with the same old evil thoughts and expect different results in our lives.

Take the white-tailed buck for example. The male deer becomes consumed with sexual desire during the rut or mating season each year. Usually the mature buck is very careful, cautious, and alert to follow his God-given instincts. Intelligently and rationally the buck uses intuition, sight, smell, and his hearing skills to alert him to any predator or danger. He is attentive to almost any minor detail that is out of place such as a foreign odor, strange scent, or obvious red flag so that he can survive. But during the rut season, his guard is let down. He cannot think clearly. He makes impulsive decisions. He chases the female in heat into dangerous or forbidden areas where he would usually never go. Once he smells the female, he has to have her even if a predator or hunter is firing arrows or shots at him.

What causes a normal male to get so sidetracked that he will pursue the prostitute sometimes into the most dangerous of places? The irrational and undisciplined man lacks self-control, and he will follow a woman into an obvious death trap hoping for temporary pleasure or just one more escapade. Proverbs 7:22 describes it like this: "Immediately he went after her as an ox goes to slaughter…as a bird hastens to the snare…he did not know it will cost him his life." I highly recommend a book by Steve Chapman called, *A Look at Life from the Deer Stand*.[10] He gives men much added perspective to this subject.

David hoped to hide or conceal his sin and ignore its built-in negative consequences. But sin is not like that. There is no way to avoid negative consequences. We always reap what we sow. We always reap more than we sow, and we always reap later than we sow.[11] Proverbs 28:13 says, "[H]e who covers his sin will not prosper, but happy is he who confesses and forsakes his sin."

Battles

Without exception, the most common story I have heard in prison is the association with the forbidden woman and how often that burning desire was the ultimate reason they ended up in the captivity of jail or prison. For King David, what began as a lustful thought led to an avalanche of bad decisions and severe consequences. The thing to remember about David was that David was a man after God's own heart. He loved God. He wrote at least seventy of the psalms that we have in our Bible. His inspired prayers and meditations are anointed by God. He conquered Goliath, killed a lion and bear, and defended the poor and the crippled, and brought hope to the common man. He loved the people of Israel and was the greatest king in Israel's history. He conquered tens of thousands of Israel's enemies and put his own life on the line time and time again for God's people. He expanded Israel's territory. But even King David, in a period of weakness, idleness, and complacency, fell prey to sexual temptation. It all began in his thoughts. If we do not kill lust, it will kill us.

Someone explained that sin begins in our thoughts like a thin crack in the windshield. It is very small, fine, almost not there, and hardly seen. Then one day, it becomes noticeable, and its growth unstoppable.

I strongly recommend Stephen Arterburn's book, *Every Man's Battle*.[12] For all of us, the spiritual battle is most often won and lost amid the sexual temptation and lust of the heart. We must fight each day's temptation by praying scripture. Pray it over and over and over:

I can do all things through Christ who strengthens me.[13]

> If God is for me, who can be against me?[14]

> Thy word have I hidden in my heart that I may not sin against God. (Ps. 119:11)

After multiple concealed and unconfessed sins, David writes about the pain and consequences of his sin in Psalms 32 and 38. He says when he kept silent about his sin, his body wasted away. He spoke of the extreme loneliness of being separated from his God. He would later pray, "God restore to me the joy of my salvation," because sin cuts off our spiritual joy. It drains away our physical, mental, and spiritual strength. When we sin, we always lose. We lose time. We lose opportunities. We lose peace. We lose power. We lose the closeness and favor of God's presence in our lives—that close-knit feeling of God with us. Satan uses sin to show us the front door to temporary pleasure but never shows us the back door. We believe the idea that sin is pleasurable, and it sometimes is; however, it always leads to greater pain and problems. Satan, the accuser, knows the battle well. He wants us to give up and give in. He wants us to simply surrender and not try to change. He tells us that this is the way God made us and that there is nothing we can do about our sinful nature. But change is possible. With God there is always hope.

Pride

Change requires that we humble ourselves, smash pride, admit our weaknesses, and daily confess our sins. It requires that we develop purity of heart. Pride is the enemy of confession. The Greek word for pride is "hubris." In classical Greek thought, "hubris" refers to arrogant and exaggerated presumption, suggesting impious disregard of the limits governing human action in an orderly universe.[15] Greek tragedies usually depict hubris or pride as the hero's tragic flaw. Pride or exaggerated self-esteem is a sin to which the great and gifted are most susceptible. Prideful people feel like they don't need anyone's help or advice. It is this same pride that caused Satan's fall from heaven, for in pride, he wanted to be equal with God (Luke 10:18). C. S. Lewis says in *Mere Christianity*, "A proud man is always looking down at things and at people; and of course, as long as you are looking down, you cannot see something that is above you." [16]

The apostle Peter, who had his own problems with pride or ego and other past failures, explained in 1 Peter 5:5 that God is opposed to the proud but gives grace to the humble. The pride of life or ego must be mortified, killed, and destroyed. Paul tells us to mortify the deeds of the flesh. If we are going to overcome sin, humility and dependence on God is step one. God's grace is the power and desire to do God's will and overcome all sin. It is God's favor and blessing. Yet pride or the refusal to bow down and acknowledge our sinfulness calls out the armies of heaven against us. The Greek word used by Peter for opposed is a Greco-Roman military term describing legions of heavenly soldiers or mighty angels lining up against the prideful person as an enemy army.

Picture Julius Caesar's legions lining up against you all alone in your pride. You would have zero chance. In essence, Peter is telling us in very clear terms that if we walk and live in pride, it is like God is calling out the armies of heaven against us. Meditate on that for just a minute. The very God we are trying to serve and worship stiff-arming us because of our independence and pride. There again, our communication with God is cut off.

Metaphorically, it is like legions or myriads, thousands upon thousands, of mighty angels lining up against us. We overwhelmingly lose. There is no chance of victory. God always wins. We often think of angels on our wings, and angels helping us along the way, but think about the armies of heavenly angels standing against us because we are walking, acting, or living in our pride.

> Everyone who is proud in heart is an abomination to the Lord. (Prov. 16:5)

We Must Think Differently

My friend Tommy was about to be released from prison after eight years. I asked him what was the first thing he was going to do when he got out. He said, "Go to the strip bar, pick up a couple of whores, get a hotel room, and get drunk." I've heard this story over and over and over. If you and I are going to be different, we must think differently.

Pride blocks positive spiritual energy. It blocks creative thinking. It blocks imagination and vision. Every form of positive energy derives itself from our Creator God. Ego zaps spiritual energy and strength. It causes one to lose balance and be in disharmony with God. We cannot walk in pride and walk with God. Our connection with the Divine is broken and our own personality, strength, and nature break down. A computer must be plugged into the power source to operate. Unplug it, and everything shuts down. It has lost contact with its source. Pride causes us to lose contact with our power source. Because of unconfessed sin, we cannot abide in Him, and the grace connection (the power to do His will) is cut off. We instantly lose favor with God.

Overcoming our own lust requires smashing pride, adding massive amounts of scripture to our memory and lots of prayers. John Calvin has said, "We must repeat the same supplications not twice or three times only, but as often as we have need, a hundred and a thousand times. We must never be weary in waiting for God's help."

Here is what I have learned, know, and have experienced about my own sin, dreams, and goals. God can do more during a short period of pain and desperate prayer to make me sweeter, kinder, stronger, more forgiving, less judgmental, more responsible, and more loving and free of lust and sin than He will do in one hundred years of easy living and no desperate prayers. Desperate problems require desperate praying and desperate connection to God.

Purity of Heart

God declared David a man after His own heart. In 2 Samuel 12:24 it is said, "[T]he Lord loved him," referring to King David. Why did God love David so much? The reason why is because David was so broken before God about his sin. He cried before God many times (Ps. 6:6, 56:8, 69:3), because David loved God so intimately. His heart was pure. His life was about prayer, praise, and worship.

Francois Muriac (a French priest) found sexual desire to be like a tidal wave powerful enough to bear all good and holy intentions. He originally taught that only "marriage will cure lust, and that true fulfillment can only be fulfilled in monogamy." He later concluded that self-discipline, repression, and rational argument are inadequate. Only in "Blessed are the pure in heart, for they will see God," does a man find freedom from lust.[17]

Impurity or lust of the heart separates us from God. It kills love. It crushes desire. It replaces our hunger for God for that which is temporary. Purity of heart keeps us connected in communion with God. In turn, our love for God overrides all else. It helps us overcome all temptation. The more we love God, the stronger we become, and we pray without ceasing (1 Thess. 5:17). This is what it means to be pure in heart. Our love for God overrides every temptation and selfish desire.

> One of the main functions of formalized religion is to protect people against a direct experience with God. (C. G. Jung)

Verse to memorize:

As a man thinks in his heart, so is he. (Prov. 23:7)

Questions for reflection/discussion:
1. What happens when we hide or conceal our sin?
2. What happens when we confess or admit our sins?
3. How does memorization and meditation of God's Word change us? Cross-reference: Psalms 51:7, 19:7; Matthew 4:4; Hebrews 4:12.
4. Why is it so important to kill the ego or pride?
5. How does God view pride?
6. List the ways we make provision for lustful thoughts and the flesh. Cross-reference: Romans 13:14.
7. What is your plan or strategy to flee lust? Cross-reference: 1 Timothy 2:2.
8. Explain what James 1:13–16 says about temptation.
9. What does God promise in 1 Corinthians 10:13 for those who face temptation?
10. Prayer is everything. Name the benefits of begging for God's mercy and crying out to Him for help.

11. What specific desires and habits do you need to ask God to help you change?
12. Name the benefits of living in a state of constant prayer?

Chapter 10: Pouring Out

The darkness of prison is felt everyday. I have seen, too often, other inmates being carted out on a stretcher officially, leaving this world and going on to the next. I have felt the empty, hollow, and sad feeling of someone's family weeping over an incarcerated family member who did not make it out of here and did not come home as he had promised. The dream of earthly freedom and reunion with family is over. I have seen and felt the depression, the loneliness, and the hopelessness. At times, it overwhelms me. I struggle to find words to express the feeling. I can only imagine what it does to God. Jesus looked upon the masses, and He was overflowing or "topped off and pouring out" with compassion for the people.[1]

It often baffles me to think of how much God loves us, and yet He restrains Himself. He holds back. He desires what power could never force: true love. He could use His power to make us all become robots who mechanically go through the motions of offering praise, worship, and adoration. But God waits for us to choose Him, and He is jealous and hurt when we choose other loves. If you have ever romantically loved someone so effortlessly where everything you do with and for the other person is perfectly selfless, then you have experienced this kind of love. Romantic love is an experience of pure grace. When your loved ones accept you, even in jail, that is pure grace. My family is full of grace toward me. I remember the first time my youngest daughter came to see me through the thick glass window of jail. On the phone I tried to tell her I was sorry for my mistakes, and she quickly and definitively held up her hand as if to say, "stop!" Then she said, "Daddy, all is forgiven. You do not have to say anything else." She is an example of God's grace.

As a Father, God is patient, giving us chance after chance to come to Him or to return to Him. He could destroy us with one thought. Instead, He weeps over us. He longs for us.

Meanwhile our flesh often demands instant miracles, signs, and wonders. We want to be delivered and set free from our confinement, and we want it now. But God's timing is rarely the same as ours, and there are no shortcuts to maturity. Yet, with this same compassion, God's loving delays are profitable, purposeful, and deliberate. To be clear, He does respond to all of our prayers all the time. He hears us cry to Him. He is near to us. He knows our pleas. He is not ignoring us, but sometimes He answers no. Other times, the answer is "not yet" because we are not ready. And of course, He longs to answer yes for us all the time, and more times than we often recognize, His answer is yes.

God's Timing

Nothing is random with God, especially His timing. In the New Testament original language, there are two words for timing. One is Kronos, which refers to history or chronology. The other is Karios, which refers to God's providential timing or a divine moment in history. When God answers prayer, it is always a Karios moment. Think of Lazarus whom Jesus loved and wept over.[2] He died and his sisters Mary and Martha were brokenhearted because Jesus did not come quick enough to heal Lazarus before he died. Let it be clear to us that there is a love that waits. Jesus delayed on purpose because Lazarus's resurrection was for a greater glory. Raising Lazarus from the dead after four days was a greater miracle than raising him from the dead after one day or healing him before he died. Everything is about God's greatest glory.

Endurance

Waiting on God means that we pray with endurance. We persevere. We keep praying even when we do not feel like it. We keep pouring out. John the Baptist's parents Zacharias and Elizabeth are another example of waiting and trust.[3] After years and years of praying and waiting on the conception of a child, the angel of the Lord told them that their petitions had been heard. They would have a son, and his name would be John the Baptist, the forerunner of the Christ, the Messiah. They had to be persistent in their prayers for many years. Can you imagine waiting on God like Zacharias and Elizabeth or as Abraham and Sarah did as they waited on the promises of God?

Prayer Quotient

In another example of prayer persistence, Jesus honored the story of a poor widow who consistently pleaded before an unrighteous judge for relief. Finally, the judge gave into her request after saying no over and over again. Jesus told the story to emphasize that our Father in heaven is much more compassionate than the unbelieving judge, but also to let us know that we should never give up in our praying. It is almost like Jesus is saying that God wants to answer our prayers with yes if He sees that we are really serious and sincere about our requests. The truth is that God honors bold and desperate praying.

Think of when Jesus was petitioned by the blind beggar named Bartimaeus to be given his sight. Jesus asked, "Do you really want to be healed?" Why would He ask that question? It appears obvious that this poor man wants to see. It is like asking people in prison if they really want to be free from this confinement. Almost all positively say yes, but there are some who really do not want to get better or change their criminal behavior patterns. Jesus knew this to be true of Bartimaeus. He knows that some people really do not want to change. One little phrase in that story tells us that Bartimaeus was sincere about transformation. It says, "He casts his rags aside and followed Christ in the way." A lot of people like their sinful past. They hold onto their past desires. In essence, they hold onto their rags instead of the responsibility required to follow Jesus. Jesus said in Luke 9:62, "No man, having put his hand to the plow, and looking back is fit for the Kingdom of God."

Looking Back

Holding onto past behaviors and attitudes is dangerous, and it signals that we really do not want to change or be healed. Lot's wife was commanded by the angel of the Lord to rush away and not look back to the sinful cities of Sodom and Gomorrah where their home was. As they made their escape, she looked back, and God turned her into a pillar of salt. "Looking back" symbolized her true nature and passions for the sinful pleasures, indulgences, and forbidden desires of the past.[4] She did not want to let go of that which God considered abominable. People often ask the question, "How could a loving, compassionate God send anyone to hell?" Jonathan Edwards, Great Awakening Preacher of the seventeen hundreds, said, "God does not send anyone to Hell. He sends sin to Hell and people hang onto it."[5]

Are We Serious about Change?

The disciples asked Jesus, "Lord, teach us to pray."[6] Of all the things they could ask Jesus to teach them, they wanted Him to teach them to pray. They saw His communication with the Father and wanted that same relationship over miracle powers, extraordinary wisdom, and a magnetic personality. They wanted to learn how to pray.

Jesus said, "Ask, and it shall be given to you. Seek and you shall find. Knock and the door will be opened to you."[7]

Again, John Calvin said, "We must repeat the same supplications not twice or three times only, but as often as we have need, a hundred and a thousand times…We must never be weary of waiting for God's help."[8]

Think of Psalms 130:5–6: "I will wait for the Lord, my soul does wait, and in His Word do I hope. My soul waits for the Lord more than the watchman for the morning." We are to have great expectations of God. Faith is demonstrated in our patient waiting and never-ending pleas for His mercy. Lamentations declares, "The Lord is good to those who wait on Him."[9]

It was written of Brother Lawrence: "Forsaking all to do everything for His love. He forgot self. He never any longer thought on Heaven and Hell or his past sins, nor on those he daily committed after he asked God's forgiveness for them. Having confessed his sins, he no more suffered his mind to go back to them, but, with confession, entered upon a perfect peace; after which he committed himself to God."[10]

Why Pray?

Some Christians have resolved themselves: "Why even pray in such a predetermined world?" If everything is going to work together for our good anyway, why is there any reason to pray? It is a valid question, especially for some people who have prayed for long periods of time, and it seems that God is not moved by their prayers.

Early church father, Origen said, "First, if God foreknows what will come to be and if it must happen, then prayer is vain. Second, if everything happens according to God's will and if what He wills is fixed and none of the things He wills can be changed, then prayer is in vain."[11] Is God a changeless God? If so, why even pray? Immanuel Kant called prayer "an absurd and presumptuous delusion" as to think that one person's prayer might deflect God's plans.[12]

But the Bible has a different view from those who might fall into prayer complacency and laziness and avoid the labor of prayer. They miss the blessedness of communication with our Heavenly Father. For me, I pray because I know God answers prayer. I know prayer changes things. I pray because I am commanded to pray. I pray because He has shown Himself strong to me through prayer. My entire Christian life I have seen the power of prayer. I have seen answers to many prayers. This is a fact that can never be argued or debated in my life. I have thirty-three years of prayer journals of answered prayers.

God tells us to pray. Jeremiah says, "Call unto Me and I will show you great and mighty things which you do not know."[13] James declares, "You have not because you ask not…and you ask with the wrong motives."[14]

Sarah, Rebekah, Rachel, Hannah, and Elizabeth were all barren. They all prayed. They all had children.

After trying to run from God, Jonah reluctantly preached to the Ninevites. God said He would destroy them in forty days. The Ninevites repented and begged God for His mercy. God relented and changed His mind. Prayer changes everything. God is the same today, yesterday, and forever. His character does not change, but God responds to the cries of His children when they appeal to His mercy and kindness. Remember George Muller's mantra: "God does nothing except in response to prayer."[15]

God has intervened throughout history when His people pray. It is like a father and his children. A child's passionate plea can change the direction and decision of a compassionate father. My children did this to me many times. When my children pled to me, I always listened, and some times, I changed my decision when I thought it was best for them. It is always too soon to quit in our prayer petitions to our compassionate Father.

King Hezekiah received fifteen more years of life on earth because he prayed after God declared through the prophet Isaiah that he was going to die. He repented of his sins, prayed, and asked God to extend his days. God changed his mind.

Martin Luther said, "I have so much business I cannot get on without spending three hours daily in prayer." Prayer changed everything for those who committed themselves to the task. Teresa of Avila explains that experiences with God through prayer are far, far more than anything we can fabricate for ourselves. The results of prayer cannot be made up!

Intense and Faithful Prayers

When a few of us in college prayed for an awakening and revival on our campus in 1988–90, God responded. Many came to Christ. The atmosphere of the place changed. It happened because of faithful people praying intense and fervent prayers. Over the next twenty years of my life, God did this over and over again. As a young minister, I had the wonderful benefit of spending time with a godly man of prayer named Robert Anderson. We prayed together almost every time we met. He taught me to always call upon the name of the Lord in everything.

When I was first incarcerated, as expected, Robert was the first person who came to my side to pray with me. The greatest revivals that occurred in my ministry always occurred during dedicated times of prayer. No one can quite explain the power of prayer to change lives, but it works. It is God's method for real change. Once again, prayer is the center of my life, and I am seeing God do wonderful things. Recently, my prayer partners and I have had the joy of leading three different inmates to the Lord. They had renounced their sins, and I had the opportunity to teach them about Christ. It is amazing to see how God answers prayers! James declares "[T]he fervent prayer of a righteous person avails much."[16] Keep praying with persistence!

Do I worry about times of absence and the silence of God during the dark period of 2011–16? I confess that I have. But not anymore. God took me through that period to teach me, retrain me, and prepare me for a greater work. I see God's hand at work over and over again every day. Never underestimate the poverty, the obscurity, and the seemingly unseen, unrewarded, unsought, and unloved places that God places us. Never underestimate the significance of service to Him even to the least of these (of which I am one). We are to bloom where God plants us and trust Him with the rest. William Carey, considered the father of modern missions and missionary to India writes, "Prayer—secret, fervent, believing prayer—lies at the root of all personal godliness."

Saving Faith

Coming to Christ is like crossing the Red Sea on dry land. We arrive at the other side with God destroying our past enemies and leaving behind the past chains of slavery and addiction. God now prepares us for His promised land. Before the promised land, we must go through the desert. We have been saved and delivered, but we are not in heaven yet. Sanctification is a lifelong process of faith that includes numerous temptations, trials, and tests.

On June 30, 1859, Charles Blondin was the first man to tightrope across Niagara Falls. Over twenty-five thousand people gathered to watch him walk some eleven hundred feet across the falls, suspended above the raging waters. There was no safety net or harness of any kind. The slightest slip would prove fatal. When he made it across, the crowd roared with enthusiasm. As the days passed, to keep the show going, he would walk across on stilts; another time he took a chair, a stove, and cooked an omelet suspended above the falls. Once, he carried his manager across riding piggyback. And once he pushed a wheelbarrow across loaded with 350 pounds of cement to many cheering spectators. Then he asked a spectator, "Sir, do you think I could safely carry you across in this wheelbarrow?" He answered, "Yes, of course." Blondin said, "Get in." Of course the man refused. He believed, but he was not ready to trust.[17]

Do we have to understand everything and have all our questions answered before we put our trust in God? No. I do not understand all there is about gravity, but I believe in it. I do not understand all there is about electricity, but I am not going to sit in the dark until I do. A relationship with God requires faith in Him.

There are three elements to saving faith: (1) knowledge, (2) belief, and (3) commitment. God wants us to enter into a covenant relationship of the purest love with Him. He wants nothing less than everything. If you have never received Christ into your life and you would like to, the best way is to voice a simple prayer of surrender to God. The words will not save you. They are simply an expression and a way to call upon God for salvation. The way to do this is to acknowledge in your heart that your sin and selfishness have separated you from Him and that you want to turn from your sin and put your trust in Him. Romans 10:13 declares that all who call upon the name of the Lord will be saved. John 3:16 says that God so loved the world that He gave His only begotten Son that whosoever believes in Him will not perish but have eternal life. In 2 Peter 3:9 it is made clear that it is not the will of God that any perish but that all come to repentance. God's love is for everyone. As you call upon the Lord, He will save you. Here is the prayer that I prayed:

> Lord Jesus. I realize that I am a sinner and that my sins have caused me to be separated from You. I ask You to forgive me of my sins and come into my heart. You are my only hope for salvation, and I call upon the name of Jesus to save me. I do not want to close the door of my heart to You anymore. I open my heart fully and completely to You. Take control of my life and help me to trust You for the rest of my life and for all of eternity. Thank you for forgiving me of my sin and giving me the gift of eternal life. Thank you for saving me. I declare that you are my Lord and Savior. In Jesus name I pray, Amen.

If you prayed this prayer in sincere faith, welcome to the family of God. You have a new heavenly family that is not going to be affected by death, divorce, separation, or abandonment. God has permanently adopted you into His family as His child to love you and be loved by you.

Do not be fearful or afraid. What God has started in your life, He will complete. Philippians 1:6 says, "For I am confident of this very thing that He who began a good work in you will perfect it until the day of Christ Jesus." You are His child, and everything, from this day forward, is working for your benefit. Everything is working together for your good and God's glory (Rom. 8:28–29).

Please do me a favor and let me know that you prayed this prayer so that I, and others, can pray for you and find ways to encourage you. You can write to my friend mentioned in the front or the back of the book, who will also write you back and send you some additional literature and information that will help you in your walk with God.

Questions for reflection/discussion:
1. Why do you think God restrains His wrath against the sins of humanity?
2. Name an example of when God has delayed in response to one of your requests.
3. Give an example of when God said no to your prayer. Why do you think He said no?
4. What are some reasons God delays or forces us to wait before He grants our petitions?
5. Describe the character and belief required to never give up in our prayers?
6. What is the difference between believing and trusting?
7. What is required for us to become part of God's family?

Chapter 11: Confinement to Conformity

Be not conformed to this world, but be transformed by the renewing of your mind, so that you may prove what the will of God is, that which is good and acceptable and perfect.
—Romans 12:2

Before I was transferred to another prison, my friend Chap and I spent many days walking laps, sharing, and praying together. Finding a prayer partner in prison makes a huge difference. Studies show that prisoners who are prayed for do much better than those who are not prayed for.

I remember a sermon I heard in the early 1990s by Pastor Jim Daniels, who preached a revival meeting for me at the beautiful church I pastored in South Carolina. He called it the formula for real change: Presentation + Transformation = Revelation. I have never forgotten it and used it many times myself to communicate how to discover the will of God. Presentation of our life to God plus the sanctifying work of transformation will make clear God's revelation. Revelation is the good, acceptable, and pleasing will of God. It is God's path for your innermost dreams and hopes. George Truett wrote, "The greatest knowledge is the will of God. The greatest accomplishment is doing the will of God."[1]

As I began writing this page, I was dumbfounded when a scar-faced inmate rudely interrupted my reading and writing and demanded that I let him hold the only copy of the Bible that was in that particular jail pod. A daily requirement of prison life is to be reminded that I have no rights—ever. I let out a deep sigh, humbled myself, and handed the Bible to him. With mean and angry eyes, he grabbed it away and ripped out a random page and then handed the Bible back to me. He said, "I need this F****** paper to roll my F****** cigarette." At sixty-two years of age, no teeth, the odor of coffee and cigarette breath, and the lack of any personal hygiene skills, he gets his kicks out of breaking the rules. He says, "I always win. I will get these GD ****** back." His negative disposition adds to the tension of an already-stressful environment.

My one-armed friend, Lucky, shared some of his wisdom with me. He says, "I consider these people as part of my rehab." Personally, I have long accepted that part of my punishment is to spend at least a portion of my day with some of the world's most irritating people. Yet, in the big picture, I must view the irritation like sand in the oyster shell before being conformed into a beautiful pearl. God uses all things, even irritating and obnoxious people.

Conformity

Conformity? How do we conform to the image of Christ? In 1872 American brothers John and Isaiah Hyatt changed the world by inventing the injection-molding process. Through this process, plastics and other materials can be heated and forced into a mold.[2] Once cooled, a perfectly formed object appears. Everyday we use or see something created by injection molding.

The two most important steps to transformation or conformity are to change the way we think and to make different the people with whom we associate. We are what we think, what we read, and what we dream. If all you think and talk about is dope and the foolishness that surrounds dope, then that is what you will continue to be. Someone has said that we are the average of the five people we spend our time with. We become like those with whom we spend our time. The Christian's goal is to let this mind be in you which was also in Christ Jesus.[3] We are to pursue peace and harmony or oneness with God. This is called abiding in Him.[4]

So how do we change our brain? How do we get our minds, which are generally conditioned for amusement, to be trained to "muse" on the will of God? The word "amusement" finds its beginnings around AD 1100. The French used the word "muse" meaning to think. "Amuse" means not to think. The etymology of the word "muse" means to stare stupidly or being absentminded. "Amusement" means to let others think for you. Most humans now grow up in front of TV, the Internet, and various media devices allowing others to do their thinking for them. I shudder to think of what I would become by feeding my thoughts a steady diet of TV, movies, talk shows, political news, and soap operas. We must change our thinking habits.

Founder of Microsoft, Bill Gates, has recently said that the entire world needs to be debugged. In essence, he describes our minds as an infected computer hard drive. We need antivirus software to detect and destroy harmful or low-energy thoughts that only bring us down. These low-energy thoughts of evil, gossip, bitterness, vengeance, and immoral passions keep us locked in unproductive and ignorant confinement. Bill Gates is right. Our minds need to be daily cleansed, erased, and wiped clean of the vanity of false concepts and low-energy thinking that stunts our cognitive skills and hinders our growth potential in Christ.

Paul explains that every thought needs to be brought into the obedience of Christ.[5] David prayed in Psalms 19:14, "Let the words of my mouth and the meditation of my heart be acceptable in Your sight oh Lord." The godly and inspired writers of the Bible understood that all sin begins in our thoughts.

If anyone knows about the power of negative and low-energy thinking, it is me. After twenty-five years of positive thinking, I fell into a depressed and impaired state. Everything went blank on me. My capacity to think clearly was diminished, and I discovered that nothing affects the mind and spirit like being consistently wrong. Everything in my life was self-destructive and irrational. For the next five years, the entire universe was against me in every single way. I lost everything. I was stripped down to nothing.

I asked a young man who had faithfully served our country as a tank operator in Iraq, yet later got caught up in a terrorist plot and a fifteen-year sentence, how prison had changed him. With sad eyes, he said, "I feel cold. After twelve years of calling home, the rejection, the criticism, rarely seeing family, I feel like I am no longer known. I am hollow and indifferent. Now, I have serious mental issues that I do not know how to resolve."

As a Man Thinks

After completing various segments of time, I always ask myself this: How am I regaining my sanity and dignity? How am I renewing my confidence? How do I prove to myself that I am getting better and not bitter? Reprogramming the mind is learned. The right habits and disciplines must be formed. My medicine has been extreme doses of God's Word as I have read the Bible through multiple times in the last five years. I have had to change my thinking and fill my thoughts with God's thoughts. While reading and praying, God brings to surface the errors of my thinking. I was able to repent and replace false assumptions that had dominated and beaten me down. I now believe God's favor rests upon me.

Someone has said that if we sow a thought, we reap an action. If we sow an action, we reap a character. If we sow a character of immoral and wrong behavior, we reap a destiny. I believe this is true. The opposite is also true. If we sow a character of Christ-likeness, we reap a destiny of peace and oneness with God, and our eternity will be full of heavenly rewards.

Romans 8:6 explains, "For the mind set on the flesh is death, but the mind set on the Spirit is life and peace." We must train our brains to kick out evil thoughts. Polluted, profane, and perverse language must be replaced with edifying words or good words that encourage and build up other people and strengthen our own faith. Negative words produce nothing. They are wasted energy. They bring curses upon our lives instead of God's favor and blessing.

Purity

The human mind begins life like a bucket of pure white paint. Over time, the mind gets tainted with illicit thoughts. The mind hears profanity, cynicism, and hostility and sees the vulgarity. The mind makes a decision to reject it or receive it. The more evil that is accepted, the quicker the mind turns from pure white to dull grey and eventually darkness. Overtime, the more we accept the impure, the darker the mind becomes. Negative and cynical thinking habits form. These evil or midnight black colors limit and kill godly thinking. Overtime, the mind becomes sin sick. The more sin, the more confused, and the more negative.

There is really no way to get the bad thoughts out of our mind. To make the bucket of paint pure, we have to add large amounts of the pure color until the evil thoughts become so diluted that they lose their effect. Unfortunately, there are some images that we will have to deal with for the rest of our lives. But the solution is to direct the mind to take the path of purity. Instead of certain vain and immoral TV shows, songs, media, magazines, and pictures, choose purity. Debug or cleanse your mind each day and take the path of a wholesome book, time in God's Word, spiritual books, history, finance, and other edifying thoughts. Refuse to take the path to low-energy, nonproductive, soul-draining thinking. It leads to repeating the same mistakes and the same self-destructive behavior. There will be no change.

Hamster Wheel

We all know what it is like to do one of three things while incarcerated: pace back and forth in a solitary cell, walk in circles in a jail pod, and walk the track at the prison. If your track is like mine, there is the track, and there is the grassy or dirt area around the track where faster joggers run to pass others who are going more slowly. There are usually several paths where hundreds of inmates walk or run in circles everyday. The paths are well worn. Our minds are the same way. There are many paths that lead to different responses. If you take the path to pornography, drugs, vengeance, and hate, that is what you will become. Instead, we must create paths in our minds that lead to peace and not conflict, hope and not despair, life and not death.

Below are three concepts to help with thinking:

1. *We attract what we are, not what we want.* The law of attraction proclaims that like is attracted to like. If you are an addict, you will attract junkies. If you are a racist, you will attract other racists. If you are negative and cynical, you will attract other low-energy thinkers. If you are a person of faith, you will attract those who long for hope. If you walk like Christ, you will naturally make a difference in those around you just like Christ did. We must eradicate the negative, destroy the ego, and develop wholesome thinking skills.

2. *We are what we think, and we are what we believe.* Our beliefs have such an effect on us that when we lose our focus, it can make us ill, depressed, discouraged, and unproductive. It is important to remember that we are not our blood cells or our DNA. Our behavior is supported by beliefs and thinking patterns. I must make a total commitment to reprogram my mind and learn the thoughts of God. Faith comes by hearing and hearing by the Word of God (Rom. 10:17). My thoughts will make or break me. My genetic make up is not my culprit. My early history and family conditioning is not my excuse. I cannot be imprisoned by my excuse inventory. Excuses must go in the trash bin. I must believe what God says I am

and nothing else. I must believe that He is always working in my favor. He always causes all things for my good. Benedict Spinoza (sixteen hundreds) wrote, "The human mind is part of the infinite intellect of God. The mind's highest goal is the knowledge of God."[6] Along those same lines, Ralph Waldo Emerson said, "What lies behind us and what lies before us are tiny matters compared to what lies inside of us."[7]

3. *Jesus is my nature and life.* He lives in me. The phrase "in Christ" is used by the apostle Paul over and over again (sixty-one times) in the New Testament. Jesus lives in me, and I have surrendered everything to Him. I am His, and He is mine. I follow Christ and no other. I have His loyalty, and He has mine. According to Acts 17:28, "For in Him we live and move and have our being." We exist only through Him.

When Christ Jesus fills us with the Holy Spirit and lives in us, then a marvelous, real change occurs. Even the most profane, angry, rude, least refined, and most selfish people transform. Their speech is different. There is a softness of voice, a tender thoughtfulness in the smallest of actions. Language changes. How we stand changes. We do not have to be first anymore. Everything changes. We are being conformed instead of confined.

Henry David Thoreau wrote, "As a single footstep will not make a path on earth, so a single thought will not make a single pathway in the mind. To make a deep physical path, we walk again and again. To make a deep mental path, we must think over and over the kind of thoughts we wish to dominate our lives."[8] Walk in His paths. Let Him show you His ways.

Action step: Remove every path that leads to destructive thinking. No unrighteous path can remain. Release the inclination to make anyone else wrong. Revoke self-righteousness and faultfinding. There is no value in blaming anyone or anything for the problems in my life.

Meditation: I am a divine creation of God. I will no longer entertain thoughts of being unworthy. My sins are forgiven. Dwelling on my pasts failures does not serve my greater good, nor God's glory. All I have is the present and whatever future God gives me. The past is gone forever. There is nothing I can do to change my past. Not even

God will change my past. My past is low-energy, nonproductive thinking.

Prayer: "Dear God, help me to never excuse or minimize my sin and its impact on my life. Help me identify the wrong meditative paths and fill my mind and time with thoughts that please You. Let the words of my mouth and the meditation of my heart be acceptable in Your sight oh Lord, my God. Turn my time in prison from doom and despair to production and prosperity."

Questions for reflection/discussion:
1. What does it mean to be conformed to the image of God?
2. Name the two most important steps to transformation?
3. Break down your typical day in prison. How much time do you spend watching TV? Talking with your friends? Fantasizing on past immorality? Looking at porn? Reading your Bible? Meditation on spiritual truth? Praying? What changes do you need to make?
4. Explain your plan to keep your mind debugged? How do you plan to keep your mind positive and full of high-energy thoughts?
5. Thoreau explains that we must make deep mental paths to the thoughts that we wish to dominate our lives? Name some of those paths.
6. What character flaws have you identified that need to be eradicated?
7. How can you build new habits to change your thinking?
8. What words, phrases, or expressions do you regularly use that need to be replaced?
9. What do I allow to fill my eyes? What does "set no wicked thing before your eyes" (Ps. 101:3) mean to you?

Chapter 12: Cries of Depression

I am weary with my groaning: All night I make my bed swim; drench my couch with my tears. My eye wastes away because of grief; it grows old because of all my enemies.
—Psalms 6:6

I have to be honest and admit with some embarrassment that there are times, even now, when I still struggle with depression. My emotions and faith waiver, and sometimes, I still question God.

Certain people exude negative energy. On one particular day, I slumped down in my plastic chair, tired of the fight and another grind of working, waiting, and hoping for something good to happen. The struggles of a long sentence and prison time left my face weary and strained. A cynical associate sat next to me and talked obnoxiously about his own obscene sentence of twenty-five years. I have heard this story over and over in endless forms by other inmates with various crimes. I fully understand his frustration. He had already served twelve hardened years and sadly lost what little accumulated good time because of drug-addiction problems. To add to his bitterness, his mother and father both passed away while he was in prison. He lost his wife to divorce. His children no longer communicate with him, and his health was in rapid deterioration due to diabetes. Only a distant sister occasionally communicated with him and put a little money on his books. He was bitter at God, bitter at the system, and bitter at the world. George Strait sings a country song about a man at a bar whose girl left him, and he hates everything. This man had the same disposition.

Unless something changes with much-needed prison reforms, he has another thirteen years to complete his time. Most people cannot comprehend one year in prison, much less decades rotting away in prison. I admit that, as a busy working taxpayer in my white-collar world, I had no idea what the average prisoner went through, and to my chagrin, I am ashamed that I did little to help the people whom Jesus called "the least of these."[1]

This man will have spent a third of his lifetime in small cages, surrounded by fences, and walls while being poked with sharp sticks by indifferent prison guards. If and when he is released, he will most likely be a ward of the state with no options but to continue in a life of crime as he will be unable to get a job and support himself.

Knowing the amount of time I had in front of me, he hissed, "Price, if I had any idea how hard the last twelve years would be, and I had the same amount of time in front of me as when I started, knowing what I know now, I would have taken a sheet, tied it around my neck to the upper railing, and jumped off the second floor in a heartbeat." After almost three years of the most intense battles of depression, I usually try to avoid this type of conversation. I know it is straight from hell and poison to my soul. Negative talk is contagious like a bad virus. But as the viper spoke, I was exhausted from the day and already a little depressed. Satan usually attacks when we are hungry, angry, lonely, or tired (HALT). It is a good time to stop and pray. Instead, I listened to his spiel. While he grumbled away, my body tensed up and began to silently shake. Instantly, my gloomy friend showed up, planting seeds of doubt and discouragement. I spent the next three days barely able to move from my bunk, questioning God's plan and my reasons to stay alive.

Personal Depression

My personal depression reached extreme levels after the failure of my securities business in 2012. I was like a walking zombie. I left everything, sincerely believing that I would never return. I eventually became a fugitive. While on the run, I spent one period of six weeks in a varmint-infested shack in which I stared at the black walls at night and the cracks of sunlight through the blacked-out windows during the day. I took nine to ten Benadryls every day to try to relieve anxiety and sleep, but nothing worked. For the first six months, I slobbered on a loaded, cocked gun barrel almost every night. I sought death, but I could not find it. I still shake as I remember those days of overwhelming disappointment. It was hard to find a reason to keep living. Only love for my family and the grace of God restrained me.

As a pastor for over sixteen years in three different churches, I counseled numerous people who were suicidal. One mother of three small children called me in the middle of the night, for an entire summer. She had been repeatedly molested by her siblings and stepfather during certain summer nights as a teenager, and it led her to a depressed and suicidal state. Thankfully she turned to Christ through prayer and survived. Another member of my church did not survive. He could not take the pressure and stress any more and took his life. I have never forgotten the phone call, nor the image. When I arrived at his house, I saw him sitting on a chair with a hose in his mouth attached to the exhaust of his car in his garage.

Few encounter depression and spiritual darkness like a prisoner. Satanic assaults, character assassinations, and distressing circumstances all contribute to a darkness that rarely lifts. There is no way to persuade a depressed person that he or she has not been rejected and forgotten by God. These feelings cause a person's IQ and cognitive abilities to contract. The need to isolate takes over quickly. Empathy from officials, professionals, or other inmates is hard to find. Compassion is nonexistent. No one ever says, "Good job," or "You are going to make it." Recently, through my cell window, I watched a dead inmate go by on a stretcher. He had committed suicide. His cellie told others that his wife had just divorced him.

Someone described hell as a place where a large banquet table of gourmet foods is always in sight. Everyone is free to eat all one wants, however, everyone's arms are replaced by an extralong fork and extralong spoon that must be used to eat. But the fork and spoon are too long to fit into the mouth. Everyone can see, smell, and touch the irresistible and delicious food, but they can't eat it. Because narcissism controls those in hell, extreme selfishness rules. There is weeping, gnashing of teeth, and bitterness. In heaven, everyone has the same fork and spoon attached to their arms, but because of love, everyone feeds each other the food. Because prison is a picture of hell, seclusion, isolation, and paranoia become the game plan.

Isolation

Stanford psychologist Philip Zimbardo in *Psychology Today* said, "I know of no more potent killer than isolation. There is no more destructive influence on physical and mental health than isolationism of you from me and us from them. It has shown to be a central agent in the etiology of depression, paranoia, murder, schizophrenia, rape, suicide, and a variety of disease states."[2]

When I first began experiencing depression, it was like playing the Whack-A-Mole game. When emotions like anger, sadness, disappointment, and grief popped up, I would whack them down as fast as I could. I would push my feelings underground and forget any expectation of hope or love. I felt that if I could crush any hopes, deny them, bury them, minimize them, and become numb to them, that my expectations for life would become nonexistent and that maybe I could die.

Pariah Woman

Some people go through some terrible things. I think of the woman who had the issue of blood for twelve years that no physician could heal, and all of her money had been used up on any and every medical possibility.[3] It was some type of chronic bleeding that was not normal, and as a result, she was isolated and quarantined from the general public. She was the scorn of society, had been written off, and there seemed to be no hope for healing or change. The Old Testament Law contains certain regulations for women with an uncontrollable flow of blood.[4] Leviticus says that such women are to be considered unclean and defiled as long as the flow of blood continued. In addition, anyone who touched such a woman would himself be seen as unclean. Everyone walked around and away from her for she was sick.

Notable teacher G. Campbell Morgan described her situation: "By the Law of Moses this woman was not allowed to touch any human being, and no human being was allowed to touch her. The Law demanded that a woman suffering in this way should be segregated. For twelve long, harsh and unbearable years this woman had been excommunicated from the Temple and the synagogue, from every religious place of assembly…she was divorced from her husband, shut out from her family, ostracized by society, and treated as a pariah."[5]

Does her story sound familiar? It does to me. I think we know a little bit of how and what she felt. The anguish of her soul and the darkness of the loneliness and rejection must have pushed her to the outer limits of insanity. In prison you long for the touch and hug of your loved ones, but godly touch and hugs are nonexistent. Studies show that infants and small children who grew up without loving touch are prone to very abnormal behavior. I wish the outside world could see what it looks like when an adult prisoner lives without touch in prison for many years. No warm embrace. No daily hugs. Honestly, I struggle to find words to describe what I see and feel. I can only imagine how many times this woman must have felt like quitting and giving up. Surely, in her suffering, she must have cried many times, "My God, my God, why have you forsaken me" (Ps. 22:1)?

Then Jesus Came

Then Jesus came. If I was delivering this message to a congregation, I would pause right there for a long time. I would have to do what I am doing right now. I would have to catch my breath, choke back my emotions, and wipe away a few tears. When Jesus came, He changed everything. Completely broken and desperate, she used her last bit of strength to push through the crowd to get as near as she could to this man they called the Healer. When she saw Him, she did the only thing she could do—she pushed. One of my inmate friends told me he was pushing in his prayers. PUSH stands for "pray until something happens." It means that you keep on praying until the light breaks through. You keep on praying, and you never quit.

She pushed, and she pressed into Him, and with whatever faith she had left, she reached out and touched the hem or the very bottom of his garment. She was so low; she was at the very bottom just like us. *For sweet reasons, the broken and crushed can always get God's attention.* He is tender toward us. I wish I could say this one thousand times because it is so important for us to know; the Bible is a story of a God reckless with desire to show you His love and get his family back.

In that moment, time stood still for her. She felt something. Power flowed from Christ to her, and instantly she was healed. Making sure His disciples understood the significance of this moment, Jesus said, "Who touched me?" Peter and the disciples did not know. They were dumbfounded. Then she fell at His feet with fear and trembling and cried. She explained her reasons and how she had been healed. Jesus said, "Daughter, your faith has made you well; go in peace." Note that Jesus called her daughter, my child—family.

When I read her brief story, I found overwhelming encouragement that Jesus cares more for us than we could ever understand. Everything happens for our good. He wants to help us, change us, heal us, and give us a firm hope. He becomes our peace. There is much we do not understand, but we must press into Him and keep pushing through these quitting points. I write this to you with tears of hope: *God can do more in one second than we can do in a trillion lifetimes.* We keep praying. We keep asking. We keep allowing Him to conform us to His will. Just like with blind Bartimaeus and this woman, Jesus stands still for us when we cry to Him!

Darkness, Signs, and Wonders

In the darkness of depression, I have learned that the God, who is with me, will also let me experience feelings of deep loneliness, shame, and suffering in such a way that I feel totally forsaken. While waiting in the darkness I have often wondered where God's miracle working power has been. God seems to go into hiding. He becomes silent. My ways are not His ways. His ways are not my ways.[6] He is mysterious. I couldn't understand His absence in my deepest pains and sorrows.

What I had to learn is that sometimes God abandons us so we will see what life is like without God. But why will He not work miracles in my situation? Sometimes He does, but most of the time He does not. Jesus, who performed many signs and wonders, said an evil generation seeks a sign.

Take, for example, the miracles, signs, and wonders that did not help the Israelites. They saw the Red Sea part. They saw the miracles of the ten plaques in Egypt. They ate miracle manna bread from heaven. They saw water come from a rock. They experienced a billion delicious quail in answer to their prayers for meat instead of manna. They saw God unleash His power in real time, right before their eyes at the tent of meeting or in the storm clouds around the Mountain of God. God gave them fire by night and a cloud to follow by day to remind them of His constant presence. He did not play hide-and-seek with them as it seems He does with us. He did not remain silent. His visible presence was with them over and over again every day. Yet, they still grumbled, complained, and were openly rebellious. They refused to thank Him. They became idolatrous, almost instantly, forgetting God's presence, power, and peace. While Moses was on the Mountain of God, they got tired of waiting for him to return with God's Word. In turn, they built a golden calf like the Egyptians, who had enslaved them, had worshipped.

     Philip Yancey brilliantly questions, "Would a burst of miracles nourish faith? Not the kind of faith that God seems interested in, evidently. The Israelites (of that time) give ample proof that signs may only addict us to signs, not to God."[7]

     So instead of signs, God gives us suffering. It does not seem fair, I know, but sufferings are better for us. God does not want us dependent on signs and wonders, or only what He can instantly give us. Instead, sufferings cause us to draw closer in love to the only reality that matters: Christ alone. We enter into His true identity, the suffering of Christ. Identification with Christ's sufferings helps us experience at least a part of what Christ and his apostles experienced; thus, we are near to Him, and He is near to us. The psalmist reminds us, "The Lord is near the brokenhearted and saves those of a contrite spirit."[8]

Following Christ

A disciple of Christ follows Christ, not men, not a church, not a person. Men will always let us down. A disciple does not follow a religion. He or she does not follow signs and wonders. A Christian follows Christ. Christianity is total adherence to Christ as Lord. Jesus's disciples abandoned their occupations and committed themselves to a very specific life and message: that Jesus Christ was crucified, buried, risen from the dead, and seen alive by over five hundred different people. They gave the rest of their lives to proclaiming this without any human or earthly profit or payoff. It was never about the money or earthly fame for them. There would be no earthly reward. Instead, they faced a life of hardship and suffering. There was a huge cost to following Jesus. Criticism would be commonplace. They accepted this life in advance. They often went without food, shelter, were ridiculed, beaten, imprisoned, and finally, most were executed in torturous ways:

- Stephen was stoned to death.
- Matthew was killed by a sword in Ethiopia.
- Mark died after being dragged by horses through the streets of Alexandria.
- Luke was hung in Greece.
- Peter was crucified upside down in Rome.
- Peter's wife was crucified beside him.
- Paul was beheaded in Rome.
- James the Just (Half brother of Jesus) was clubbed to death in Jerusalem.
- James the son of Zebedee was beheaded by Herod Agrippa I in Jerusalem.
- Bartholomew was beaten to death in Turkey.
- Andrew was crucified on an X-shaped cross in Greece.
- Thomas was repeatedly stabbed to death in India.
- Jude was killed with arrows.
- Barnabas was stoned to death.

The list of early church martyrs goes on and on.

Why? For what reason? Because they had good works in mind or good intentions? No. They were convinced without a shadow of a doubt that they had seen Jesus crucified, buried, and be raised to life. If Jesus conquered death, He will open doors to eternal life and peace for you and me. They could not resist the amazing appeal of the person of God in all His glory. Once they tasted of the pure connection to God through abiding in Christ, nothing else mattered to them.

Moreover, Christ's resurrection gave them all the hope they needed for their own resurrection. If we have the hope of our own resurrection through an abiding relationship with Jesus, then there can be no more depression. We can overcome everything. We can do all things, and if God is for us, who or what can be against us? Theologian Thomas Aquinas has said, "True peace consists in not separating ourselves from the will of God."[9] Drawing as intimately close to God as is humanly possible is the answer to every doubt, fear, and anxiety we will ever face in prison or life.

Felicity

Felicity was a servant of Christ in AD 200. She was executed because she refused to renounce her faith. She died in peace praising God as she was placed in an arena with a wild bull who crushed and killed her. The word "felicity" means God's tranquility personified. It expressed an important attitude: it is this all-consuming desire or affection for being close and at peace with God.

C. S. Lewis wrote these words after his wife died of cancer: "Meanwhile, where is God? This is one of the most disquieting symptoms. When you are happy, so happy that you have no sense of needing Him…you will be, or so it feels, welcomed with open arms. But go to Him when you are desperate, when all other help is vain, and what do you find? A door slammed in your face, and a sound of bolting, and double bolting on the inside. After that, silence. You may as well turn away. The longer you wait, the more emphatic the silence becomes."[10]

While in solitary I spent a lot of time on my knees praying for God to come through for me. It was a most difficult time. When I needed comfort, it seemed there was none. There were times when there were no more tears to cry and no more words to pray.

On the hundredth day in solitary confinement, I started seeing the glory of God in ways I had never seen before. Glory is hard to define, but you know it when you see it and feel it, and you know it is only in the most intimate connection to God that you see it. For example, when the sun sets in a display of indefinable color, or when you look at the life's work of an unparalleled artist, or when you stand staring so intensely at the ocean that you can see where it meets the sky on the horizon and you say, "That's glorious!" Glory implies that something is totally unique or different from everything else and is worth admiration. It is synonymous with being in awe of something.

A Mystery Explained

While in the hole, I meditated on the book of Isaiah. The Old Testament prophet Isaiah explained a mystery of God's glory for me: "For a brief moment I will abandon you, but with *deep compassion*, I will bring you back" (emphasis added). In Isaiah, God says, "I am Your creator. You were in my care even before you were born."[11] Because God cares about us so much, there are times that He abandons us to our folly and sinful ways for our own good. As we read the Old Testament prophets, we see that God is a jealous, lovesick Father who is repeatedly betrayed by His own people who love to worship idols and other gods.

We are prone to wander from God and forget His faithfulness to us. We often chose sin, wickedness, and idolatry over gratefulness and faithful service to Him. Like a jilted lover, sometimes God is ready to severely discipline us because of our sins, but He is always restrained by His compassion. Dietrich Bonhoeffer scribbled a note in a Nazi prison camp, "[O]nly the suffering of God can help."[12] In His goodness and mercy, He lovingly corrects us. We may feel abandonment and depression. We may feel sorrow and sadness. We may feel anxiety and worry. But in the suffering and darkness, He allows us to draw close to Him, identify with Him, and know Him intimately. That is when the depression turns to glory. Annie Dillard states, "You do not have to sit outside in the dark. If, however, you want to look at the stars, you will find that darkness is required. The stars neither require it nor demand it."[13]

Just As I Am

In 1822 a young woman named Charlotte Elliot was visiting some friends in the west end of London. There she met a minister of the gospel named Dr. Cesar Malan. Over the meal, he asked her if she was a Christian. When she replied she did not want to talk about the subject, Dr. Malan replied, "I did not mean to offend you, but I want you to know that Jesus will save you if you turn to him." Several weeks later they met again, and she said that she had been trying to come to Christ but did not know how to do it. Dr. Malan said, "Just come to Him as you are." Taking his advice, she composed a poem that began this way:

> Just as I am, without one plea,
> but that Thy blood was shed for me,
> And that Thou biddest me come to Thee,
> O Lamb of God, I come, I come!

Twenty-seven years later in 1849, William Bradbury set the words to music. Since then it has become one of the most loved hymns of all time. Billy Graham has ended all his crusade messages with the singing of "Just As I Am." The third verse contains Charlotte Elliott's testimony:

> Just as I am, though tossed about,
> with many of conflict, many a doubt,
> Fightings and fears within, without,
> O Lamb of God, I come, I come!

Prayer: "My God and King, may my heart never leave the treasures you give me in suffering. May I relinquish all selfish desires and be content in you alone. Nothing else. Thank you for correcting me and transforming me. In your loving and forgiving arms I am completely fulfilled. Amen."

> There are times in which a genius would wish to live. But it is not in the calm stillness of life or the reprise of the pacific station that great character is formed. The habits of a vigorous mind are formed in contending with difficulties. (Abigail Adams)

Questions for reflection/discussion:
1. Describe what kind of commitment and dedication it takes to spend hours each day immersing yourself in the Word of God?
2. Why is it important to thank God in our affliction?
3. Name some ways you can look for God's plan in your pain?
4. Share some results of the last time you prayed and fasted.
5. Why do you think God abandons us yet with deep compassion brings us back?
6. What does suffering help us accomplish?

> *Let the groaning of the prisoner come before you; according to the greatness of Your power; preserve those who are appointed to die.*
> —Psalms 79:11

You number my wanderings; Put my tears into Your bottle;
Are they not in Your book?
—Psalms 56:8

Chapter 13: Seasoned by Fire

Blows that hurt cleanse evil as do stripes the inner depths of the heart.
—Proverbs 20:30

I met Roberto in prison. He was serving a life sentence for murder that got reduced to thirty years. He smiled at me when I asked him if he knew Christ as his Lord. He pointed to a long nasty scar on his neck where he had been assaulted while in prison. Three years earlier, while serving food to other inmates in what is called the SHU (special housing unit) or "shoe," a unit that houses prisoners for disciplinary reasons, he was stabbed in the neck by another inmate through the food slot. He had bent over to hand a tray of food when the hostile inmate furtively reached out and sliced a three-inch gap into his neck. Bob lay on the floor and almost bled out before someone rescued him at the last minute. Not long after that his life changed.

He spoke to me with a strong Latin accent, "I was in prison for the third time, in a gang and doing stuff in prison that was worse than what I did on the streets. I was in terrible pain with this huge gash that missed my juggler by a centimeter, and now it was infected. Death would have been so welcome at that moment." He winced at the memory, "I've come to realize that pain and conflict always seem to welcome death. All I wanted to do was escape the physical and mental pain." He went on, "I was sick of living, sick of my life, and sick of the misery. I hated prison. I hated the guards. I hated our government. I knew that if I survived and got released one day, I would be repeating the same stupid stuff. My life was all about myself, pleasure, getting high, and controlling others. I wanted to be king of the yard. It is all about sin and ego, and it all leads to the same end: misery, pain, ruin, separation from friends and loved ones, and then you die a lonely death. You look back at your life and realize that you did little good and a whole lot of bad, and now you must face judgment—all alone."

I nodded slightly and asked, "So what happened?"

Bob said, "I lived. A few days later, I met another inmate; a career criminal with no hope of ever being released. He had multiple life sentences because he killed a federal agent and had some other murders connected to his crime. He was seventy-five years old and was the gentlest, sweetest, and happiest person I'd ever talked with. He had no worries, ran six miles a day, and was in perfect health. To him, life was beautiful and good. He had spent over twenty-five years in maximum security, playing the games of prison. When he was sixty-eight years old, he learned the gospel and became a believer.

"When I met him the first time, he promised to pray for me, and little by little, I began to want to know the difference in his attitude. He invited me into his little cell, and we talked for hours and hours about Christ and the amazing power of love, forgiveness, and God's grace. I knew I needed forgiveness because my heart was full of sin. I had studied other religions, but none of them had a real plan for forgiveness and love. I needed love so I could give love. I hated everybody everywhere. I hated America, and I hated my adversaries. I could not forgive anyone, smile, show kindness in any kind of way. Hate and anger ruled my life. So finally, I prayed. I asked Christ into my heart and received His forgiveness. I confessed my sin and invited God to lead me to make things right. I began to read the Bible for hours every day. I learned how to daily kill sin in my life. My life quickly changed. Overwhelmingly, the old Bob died, and the new Christ-centered Bob took over."

I asked, "And now? How are you doing your time?"

He said, "With a brand-new outlook. My hope and faith are in Christ, and no matter how bad this place is, and it is filthy bad in every way, I understand that this is not my home. I surround myself with truth tellers. I want no deception of any kind as it only invites contaminants into my life. No toxins of ungrace and judgment. All these things fester, infect, and destroy me. I must constantly purify my thoughts with God's truth. It is His truth that sets me free!"

About three months later, I watched Bob walk out the front gate with no cuffs, no chains, a bus ticket, and seventy-five dollars in his pocket. He was headed to the halfway house after twenty-seven years of federal prison a changed man. The last I heard he was back in Missouri with his family with a new job and a new lease on life. God loves to extend grace, favor, and compassion to people whom society has written off.

Transformation

For all of us still here, the cold reality of prison time is that it is brutally painful. We feel ashamed and embarrassed that our lives have come to this. Every time we make a contact with anyone outside prison, our family is reminded through some recording or notice that we are prisoners. We've made mistakes, and poor choices and the consequences have brought us to a place of great adversity. Psychologically, we are beaten up each day with constant condemnation in a social environment of negative, addictive, drug-seeking drama. The entire process of confinement is painful. Why are we here? Why has God brought us to this place? Frederick Douglas once said, "If there is no struggle, there is no progress."[1]

God wounds us to heal and help us. The psalmist says, "Before I was afflicted I went astray, but now I obey Your Word."[2] One of the purposes of affliction is to teach us things we would never have learned otherwise. Note what Bob said. He finally got into God's Word. He finally started praying. He finally started learning that life was much more than himself, but it did not happen until he was stabbed in the neck and almost dead from infection. He reached for hope at the last minute. We all must face the test of a hopeless situation.

One of the many fascinating events in nature is the emergence of the cecropia moth from its cocoon. It is an event that occurs only with much struggle and adversity on the part of the moth to free itself. The story is told of someone who watched the moth go through this struggle. In an effort to help, not realizing the necessity of this struggle, the observer snipped the shell of the cocoon. Soon the moth came out with its wings all crimped and shriveled. But as the person watched, the wings remained weak. The moth, now doomed to crawling out of the cocoon in a brief life of frustration and paralysis, even being the beautiful creature God created it to be, would soon die. The fight to emerge to freedom is an essential part of developing the muscle system of the moth's body and pushing the body fluids out into the wings so they expand. God made the struggle or adversity to make the moth healthy and strong. By unwisely interfering with the moth's struggle by cutting it out, the moth was crippled and then doomed.

Prison is full of stress, struggle, and suffering. The long waiting process takes a toll on every part of our body and mind; however, God knows how much time we need. He knows when we have had enough and when we are ready to be freed from this cocoon. He knows how much discipline or correction he wants us to experience so that we can become a better, more Christ like person. God is building spiritual and mental muscle through the adversity. We can be confident that when we submit to God's perfect will, He will mold and build a beautiful person of character.

Some Never Change

As I was writing this, I met a seventy-nine-year-old inmate named Chuck. In thirty seconds I sized him up. Mean, bitter, and full of the ego, he had been in prison off and on since 1956 when he joined the army. He went AWOL at eighteen and began a long life of crime. He is close to finishing another ten-year federal sentence for sexual assault on a minor. He had a coffee cup that had a US Army sticker on it. I completed basic and advanced training and time serving in the Army National Guard right out of high school. His mouth spieled of vulgar, bitter, and hateful words accented by "GD" at the beginning, middle, and end of each sentence he unwittingly tried to formulate. His life is sad. Stuck in intellectual ignorance and confinement, he has spent years and years in prison and has experienced no change, no healing, and even now, no hope. He only sought to stay high and play prison games. He never wanted to change. When he is soon released, he has no family, no friends, and no place to go.

Otto Dibelius, German theologian, said, "God does not lead His children around hardship, but leads them straight through hardship. But He leads. And amidst the hardship, He is nearer than ever before."[3] Because of God's presence, favor, and blessing, we can do all things through Christ.[4] We can keep a happy and positive attitude even when our appeals are turned down and our courts neglect to give us relief. Even in the extreme claustrophobia of small holding cells in chains with no room to breathe or even turn around, we can overcome. Even when we sit in dark cells for months in lockdowns and do not see the sunshine, hear a bird sing, or feel a gentle breeze, we can endure through and for Christ. If God is for us, who can be against us?[5] In spite of the obstacles and adversity, sufferings produce perseverance that enables us to pursue goals of wisdom, patience, and grace to minister to the most difficult and hideous people. We all know that if we can endure prison, we should have no problem enduring difficult people in the free world. We must believe this adversity will one day be the wind at our back.

Extreme Stress

Pioneer missionary J. Hudson Taylor who founded the China Inland Mission was caught up in the Boxer Rebellion when missionaries were being captured and killed in China. He went through such agony of the soul that he said he could not even pray. Writing in his journals, he summarized the agony of his spiritual condition this way: "I can't read. I can't write. I can't pray. But I can trust."[6] We have all experienced the intense times when the darkness of jail and prison will not lift no matter how much we pray. I have been there. I have begged and pleaded and politely asked and let my voice be heard before the Lord. I have called upon His name over and over again and learned I can trust Him. It is not that He does not hear me. It is not that He can't change my situation. It is just that He knows I need the stress to make me stronger. Just like we stress our muscles, so God stresses our faith. A. W. Tozer once said, "It is doubtful that God can use a man greatly until He has hurt him deeply."[7]

God is still working in me. The apostle Paul explains that God who began a good work in me will complete it until the day of Christ Jesus.[8] God is in me, with me, and for me. If He is for me, who can come against me except by His will. That tells me that all things are working together for my good to conform me to the image and person of Christ even in the darkness of prison.[9] In fact, I am predestined to become like Him no matter how much sin, suffering, sadness, and sorrow I go through. In Mark 9:49, Jesus says that everyone will be seasoned with fire.

The word "providence" has two parts—its "pro" and "video" put together, literally meaning "to see before." It refers to God's gracious oversight of the universe. Not only does God know the big picture or the view from above but He also knows the tiniest of details. He makes no mistakes. R. C. Sproul emphasizes, "God does not roll the dice,"[10] meaning nothing ever happens by chance. When

God causes "all things" to work together, He means even the smallest details of how long we wait in a solitary cell.

Darkness Is Required

Joseph was sold into slavery by his brothers. He then spent thirteen years in Pharaoh's prison before he finally was promoted to the palace and eventually became second in command of the entire world. A worldwide famine came, and Joseph met his brothers who betrayed him and came to Egypt in need of food. It was then that Joseph, speaking to his murderous brothers and choking back tears, firmly declared to his brothers that what they meant for evil, God used for good. You may have committed your crimes as I did with no evil intent. I know that my crimes had no evil or malicious intent. I will stand on that fact all the way through eternity, no matter what anyone may think or believe. Regardless, evil happens to everyone in some form or fashion, and what some may mean for evil, God still uses for good. If I am trusting God, I know that I am going to experience God's very best for me. His very best for me always brings out the greatest joy and peace that I can possibly stand in this body of flesh. When this happens, we will always be able to say, "I would not change my circumstances even if I could because I can now see what God's beautiful plan was all about."

Certainly there are many times in prison when we feel forsaken and very lonely. Family and even our closest and most beloved friends forget us. It is a common story. We ask and pray along with the psalmist, "My God, My God, why have you forsaken me?"[11] Eventually, God makes it clear that He has not left us, and He will not accept our letter of resignation, no matter how many times we try to turn it in. Believe me, in the midst of my depression, I have tried several times to end things my way. But God expects us to get up, keep working, and keep believing. He pursues us and will never relent. He finds us, calls us, refines us, rebukes us, encourages us, and refits and repots us. Then He commissions us for His work all over again.

Surely Joseph had moments in his thirteen years where he had to have prayed, "God, hurry up. I am so ready to get out of here!" But God is in no hurry to promote us to a higher position of influence until we are ready. We must bloom where we are planted.

Remember this is a waiting place, not a wasted place. Have you ever noticed how corporate America likes to promote rising stars too fast? Through Christ, we are all rising stars, but we must first learn to serve God in obscurity.

Obscurity

Dr. C. I. Scofield once said, "There are two tests of service to our Lord. One is the test of obscurity, and two is the test of popularity."[12] Can we serve in little-known places—obscure jobs like cleaning toilets, showers, cutting grass, laundry, and taking out the trash? I know about the test of obscurity. I was once called a backwoods preacher because I served in small obscure places. I know what it is like to preach to twenty people in small churches, but I also know what it is like to preach in front of five thousand people. I also know what it is like to be successful. I ran a successful investment-advisory business with over seven hundred clients, and now that my business has failed, I once again know what it is like to be the bum of the world and live in absolute isolation, alienation, and obscurity.

King David knew obscurity. After the fame of killing Goliath and leading Israel to many victories, he became hated by the despotic king Saul. He spent thirteen years running for his life. He lived in caves and in the wilderness, and before being anointed as king, David lived and worked in shepherd's fields.

Moses began his ascension to leadership with a fight and a murder, and then spent forty years of waiting on God to come through for him. Finally, God spoke to him and called him while he was on the backside of the desert. Certainly there were times when Moses was exhausted while waiting on God. He was eighty years old before he began leading the children of Israel through the Red Sea and eventually to the promise land at the Jordan River fulfilling his life mission. Martin Luther King said, "Christianity has always insisted that the cross we bear precedes the crown we wear."[13]

Paul spent the first three years after his conversion to Christ in Arabia with other Christians and in solitude before he launched the most successful missionary work within the history of the church. God almost always does a deep, life-changing work in us privately before He uses us publicly. For us, and I know it sounds impossible with all the noise, prison can be that place of solitude, reflection, and life-changing work. Look at your situation as God giving you a great opportunity—a second chance to get things right.

Solitude

Here are some of my favorite quotes on solitude:

> Conversation enriches the understanding, but solitude is the school of genius. (Ralph Waldo Emerson)[14]

> I have discovered that all unhappiness of men arises from one single fact: they cannot stay quietly in their own chamber. (Blaise Paschal)[15]

> I live in solitude which is painful in youth, but delicious in the years of maturity. I lived in solitude in the country and noticed how the monotony of a quiet life stimulates the creative mind. (Albert Einstein)[16]

Here is the bottom line: every trial is like a job interview—God promotes time-forged character that has been tested and tried through much adversity, solitude, and suffering. You and I have been kicked in the teeth in the worst way. In many cases we must accept the burden of over punishment. We have some kind of blemish on our record, and we have lost trust in our respective worlds. We have to earn it back little by little. Most people will not believe in our progress. The world is full of haters. They will call it jailhouse religion. They know us by our mug shots and the negative and biased media reports of our criminal history. Many of our press and media reports wrongly define our crimes and take our stories entirely out of context. But it's OK. With God's help, we will overcome! God gives us renewed confidence. His Word becomes our word. His thoughts become our thoughts and meditation.

Thoreau has said, "I know of no more encouraging fact than the unquestionable ability of man to elevate his life by a conscious endeavor."[17] For me, that conscious endeavor is extended times of devoted prayer. I believe that as we learn to communicate with God, He changes us and changes everything for His glory. We may have to labor for Christ in a very unrewarding environment for longer than we want. We may serve others for Christ in obscurity and adversity, unpaid, unloved, unsought, and unknown. That's OK. Rejoice. Give thanks. Our trials are building patience.[18] Our reward is God's beautiful presence and the conscious awareness that He brings to our lives what is far better than any pleasure even in the free world. God is pleased with secret, simple, specific, and sincere prayers of faith. We must see prison as a place for God to help us repent, kill the ego, and transform the inner self that is dominated by selfishness. As for me, I know that if I survive this passage of time and adversity, the failures of my past will fade away and become the wind at my back rather than the driving gale that has been in my face. I believe God can do the same for you.

Pray Psalms 71:20–21: "You who have shown me many troubles and distresses will revive me again and bring me up again from the depths of the earth. May you increase my greatness and turn to comfort me."

Questions for reflection/discussion:
1. What is the purpose of our struggles and pain?
2. List the habits, behavior, thinking patterns that you believe God wants you to change?
3. Describe the test of a hopeless situation you have faced?
4. What do you do when you meet people who spill negative energy?
5. Define desperate praying.
6. Why does God use darkness and obscurity to kill our egos and get us to surrender?
7. Name some benefits of solitude. Where is your quiet place for your quiet time with God?
8. What does it mean to be seasoned with fire? Cross-reference: Mark 9:49.

Chapter 14: Passion for God

Passion always overcomes excuses. After all the beat downs, disappointments, and depression, it can be difficult to find passion, but we must remember that we can do all things through Christ. If God is for us, who can be against us? God tells us to pray and to draw near to Him. If we abide in Him and His words abide in us, we can ask anything we wish, and it will be done for us. Nothing is impossible as long as it is within the will of God.

     A growing passion and enthusiasm signifies God is in us, with us, and for us. He is our force and our energy for transformation to live in His abiding presence. We don't need ego or the pursuit of the alpha-male syndrome. We need to simply walk in the bliss of God and know His presence in every waking moment, even when we are disappointed by our trials and sufferings.

     James, the half brother of the Lord Jesus, lived in a time of great persecution and suffering. He would soon die for His Lord. Before his death he proclaimed, "Consider it pure joy, my brethren, when you face various trials knowing that the testing of your faith builds perseverance!"[1] Consider trials pure joy. As Mother Teresa liked to say, think of sufferings as kisses from Jesus.[2] Problems are for our good, and they mean that God really loves us. Think of your pain with enthusiasm. Give thanks and rejoice in all things. Passion is synonymous with God. God is for us, with us, and in us! There should be nothing that you are not willing to do or think on to become what God has destined you to be.

I've Been Looking for You All My Life

One of my many cellmates—I have had forty-nine over the past three years as of this writing—was forty years old and had spent most of his adult life in both state and federal prisons. He just started a new fifteen-year sentence on gun-related charges. Not long ago he received a letter from someone he did not recognize. He opened the letter with great anticipation. Three pictures of a bright-eyed, blond-haired, teenage girl fell out of the letter. A minute later, he yelled, "Holy S***!" He read the letter and then smiled broadly, threw it over to me, and said, "Read this."

I read the first two sentences. Immediately, a lump formed in my throat. By the time I read the third sentence, the lids of my eyes could not contain the tears that I tried to restrain. It was impossible. I asked him for permission to publish the letter, and he acquiesced:

> Dad? Hey, its your daughter ******. I've been looking for you all my life. When I found out you were my dad, and where you were, I got so happy. I knew you existed! No one would tell me anything about you or even if you were alive. I have always wanted to meet you and see you. I'd love to get to know you. I want to tell you a little about myself. My entire name is ***** *******. I love coffee, tattoos, basketball, football, and so much more. I am fifteen years old now. LOL. All grown up I guess. I am in the ninth grade. High school is a little harder than I thought it would be, a lot of peer pressure. I've always wondered what you are like. What is your favorite color? Football team? Etc. I really want to get to know more about you. By the way, my favorite team is the Gamecocks and the Panthers. Well, I am going to get ready for dinner. Have a good day, daddy. Please write back as soon as possible. Here is my cell phone number if you want to call me. Most important, I love you no matter how many mistakes you've made, and I will always be here for you. Don't ever forget that. If you ever need me, call me at that number. I am going to write you every week now that I know who and where you are.

This particular cellie had been in and out of prison for only a few brief stints since he was eighteen years old. Being the "tomcat" that he is, he is unsure of how many children he has. He smirks as he says he has multiple "baby mommas." His daughter's letter started out with "Dad," followed by a question mark. She was unsure, insecure, yet hopeful that it was her dad. She had been looking for him all her life. She was lovesick for her absentee father. As I read that, I immediately thought of Psalms 68:5 which says, "God is the Father to the fatherless." God created us, adopted us, and is lovesick for us.

For those of us with children and grandchildren, we carry the heaviest of burdens. At times, we feel like failures with no remedy or recourse. God put an internal instinct in us to be providers. I have often felt sick that my hands are so tied that I cannot make money to provide for my family. It is a heavy load that I often carry.

We are to mimic the character of God and be an example to our children of what the Heavenly Father is like. The guilt and shame of not being able to fulfill those responsibilities rip the heart right out of our chests. More than anything else, we are no longer physically present while God has always promised to be there for us, no matter where we are or what we are going through.

As a father, for eighteen years in a row, I rarely missed a night of prayer with my children. It was just a habit that I developed early on to spend a few minutes praying over them as they went to sleep each night. I can think of nothing that would bring me greater joy than to take one of my children, my wife, or my mother to dinner, just the two of us, and look intently into their eyes and listen to their greatest fears, dreams, and hopes. It sends waves of pleasure down my spine just thinking about it.

Unfortunately, we cannot be there when our sons and daughters are hurt, sick, heartbroken, or sad. For many of us, we are not there when they become teenagers, learn to drive, start to date, get an award at school, play in a ballgame, graduate, work their way through college, get married, and have children themselves. I listen to the most sorrowful stories. With flat and hollow eyes, my current cellie told me how his mother and father, both in their early fifties, died while he was in prison. I listened to another inmate tell of how his son was killed in an accident the other day, and there was nothing he could do. The chaplain's office gave him a free thirty-minute phone call, and that was it. The prison system usually does not let an inmate attend a funeral. One time, at prison visitation, I watched another friend bent over and weeping in his chair for four hours while his mother consoled him on his father's passing away. He shared with me the sad reality that he never reconnected to his father after years of bitter conflict. Throughout his entire life, he never heard his dad say, "I'm sorry," and he never heard his father say, "I was wrong."

In prison, we know what it is like to feel abandoned and all alone. We feel the anguish, sadness, and emptiness. However, our children feel it even more. They long for us with lovesick hearts. With amazing grace, they are quick to forgive us. Except for those who have been intentionally hurt and abused; they fight for us to find a way to return to them as soon as possible. They need us and miss us with everything in their being.

Scott Peck wrote in his book, *The Road Less Traveled*, "All children are terrified of abandonment, and with good reason. This fear of abandonment begins around the age of six months as soon as the child is able to perceive itself to be an individual, separate from its parents. For with this perception of itself as an individual, comes the realization that as an individual it is quite helpless, totally dependent and totally at the mercy of its parents for all forms of sustenance and means of survival. To the child, abandonment by its parent is equivalent of death."[3]

Why We Keep Passionately Praying

I celled for a short period of time with a young father who had killed his baby son. He was dope sick and left with the responsibility to watch and care for his four-month-old. His son had a dirty diaper, was very hungry, and would not stop crying. Coming off a meth high with no immediate fix, he lost his temper and shook his little baby to death. In jail he had massive psychological issues as he faced a long sentence. His regret was immense. He cried real tears to me: "I wish I had my son back."

Frederick Buechner tells this true story in one of his sermons:

> It is a peculiarly twentieth century story, and it is almost to awful to tell: It is about a boy of twelve or thirteen, who, in a fit of crazy anger and depression, got hold of a gun somewhere and fired it at his father who died, not right away, but soon afterward. When authorities asked the boy why he had done it, he said that it was because he could not stand his father because his father demanded too much of him, because he was always after him, because he hated his father. And then later on, after he had been placed in a house of detention somewhere, a guard was walking down the corridor late one night when he heard sounds from the boy's room, and he stopped to listen. The words that he heard from the boy sobbing out in the dark were, "I want my father. I want my father.[4]

Maybe in your distress, you have killed your relationship with your Heavenly Father. Bitterness has consumed you. You shook your fist at Him and cut off all communication. Know this: He lovingly and patiently waits for you. We need our Heavenly Father.

How Are We Changing?

Our families need us. They need us to finish our GEDs, vocational programs, continuing education, anger management programs, drug abuse, and rehab programs. They need us to keep fighting our cases and finding ways to get our time down. They need us permanently clean from drugs and crime and to never hurt another person or ourselves the rest of our lives. They need us to develop skills to reenter the world with a professional career and job skills we have never had before. They need us to be educated and grow in extraordinary knowledge, wisdom, and understanding. They need us to develop a broad vocabulary without profanity, which is the language of the ignorant. They miss us. They love us. They want us.

They need to believe in us because we have found peace and healing from our illnesses and disorders. They need to know that we have corrected abnormal behavior and that ego no longer drives our lives. They need to know that we have learned to effectively communicate to all people with a calm and respectful demeanor. They need to know that we can control our tempers, exercise patience, hold a job, and that we have the vision, skills, and confidence to function within the laws of our land. They need to see a godly man of prayer who is on mission to change his world for good. They need to see us paying our debts and taxes, doing right, and living in integrity. They need to see us doing what we say we are going to do, telling the truth, and they need to know with confidence that whatever time we have left, when we finally get out of this hell hole, we are going to devote ourselves to their success. We are not going to miss any more ball games, recitals, ceremonies, holiday gatherings, vacations, date nights, or walks in the park. We are going to be sober for the holidays and birthdays, and everyday, because we are commanded to be not drunk with wine or any drug, but to be filled with the Spirit of God.[5] They will know that God has changed us into men of God who passionately love God, love other people, and who are absolutely, utterly, totally, and completely lovesick for our children and families.

Teresa of Avila admonishes, "It is essential, I maintain, to begin the practice of prayer with a firm resolution to persevere in it."

The prophet Malachi declares, "Behold, I am going to send Elijah the prophet (the New Testament John the Baptist) before the coming of the great and terrible day of the Lord. He will restore the hearts of the fathers to their children and the hearts of the children to their fathers, so that I will not come and smite the land with a curse."[6] The Spirit of Elijah has come, and Jesus has restored all things. Through Him there is forgiveness, second chances, healing, and hope.

Our Children Watch Us

Our children have been looking for us all our lives. Unfortunately, many of us have checked out. We left without saying good-bye and telling them when we were going to return. Some of us have chased a bottle, the needle, the pills, the prostitutes, "easy money," and worldly pleasures while sacrificing our family and neglecting our responsibilities as a parent. Some of us have crawled into a bottle, even in prison, and we are unable to get out. Our families have heard our blubbering and broken promises to quit over and over again only to see us continue to self-destruct. They need to hear that we are still trying. They need to hear that we are attending and following our AA/NA programs. They need to hear that we are "disciplinary or shot-free." They need to hear that we are coherent and focused on new goals and dreams.

Our children need us to communicate with them and not be silent. So many prisoners choose to hide. One friend of mine has not called his children in ten years. Another has not had a visit in twelve years. Other stories are too sad to tell.

With us being gone from their lives, there is an empty space that cannot be filled by any other earthly substance or personality. It is the way God made each of us. Children long for their daddy's blessing. The hole in their hearts can only be filled by us. No one else can fill that hole. Our presence, not "presents," is required. We are to be there, and we are to be with them "clothed and in our right mind." Receive and live in the grace of God!

New Beginnings

It is true, we cannot go back to a new beginning and start over, but we can start now and make a brand-new end.

Meditate on Carl Sandburg's poem "Prairie":

> I tell you the past is a bucket of ashes.
> I tell you yesterday is a wind gone down,
> a sun dropped in the west.
> I tell you there is nothing in the world,
> only an ocean of tomorrows,
> a sky of tomorrows.[7]

Forget the past. Isaiah 43:18–19 says, *"Do not call to mind the former things or ponder things of the past. Behold, I will do something new"*. It is not so important how we start the race, but how we finish the race. I was a state champion miler and two-miler in high school. I always started the four- and eight-lap races toward the back of the pack of runners. I loved to come from behind and win the race. Being in prison instantly puts us in the back of the line. We have to fight our way back to the front, and if you keep trying, you are not failing. The only way we fail is when we give up. God is honored when we keep programming even when our case managers, counselors, and other staff do not recognize our efforts. Never give up. Pray your way to peace. Passionate persistence and perseverance will pay off.

God does not want us to waste this time. We do the possible. God does the impossible. With Christ all things are possible, even restoring the most broken and dysfunctional relationships. Nothing is impossible with God, including that much-prayed-for early release. God knows when we are ready to leave prison, and when He says the word, it will be done.

What God values most is our passionate love for Him. He does not force love, but He makes it clear: "All things work together for good for those who *love Him* and are called according to His purpose".[8] Give yourself passionately to Him and His purposes.

The overcrowding of our prisons and mass incarceration efforts of our government is evidence that our world needs awakening and revival. Revival must always begin with me. It does not begin with anyone else. Its me, oh Lord, standing in the need of prayer. When God begins to move, it is absolutely phenomenal to witness. You cannot stop it because you did not start it. You cannot explain it because you did not manufacture it. You cannot duplicate it because you did not create it. Lost people are saved. The saved are revived. Fathers turn their hearts toward their children. Doors open. Doors close. Miracles happen. Those things that are dead are brought back to life. Sanity is restored. Forgiveness is granted. Confession of sins is made. Vision is given. God shows Himself strong on our behalf and does far more beyond our greatest hopes and dreams. It is time for a passionate turning of our hearts and love to Him.

> You have made us for Yourself, Oh Lord, and our hearts are restless until they rest in you. (St. Augustine)[9]

Prayer: "Lord, now I give myself to You. You are able to do far more abundantly beyond all that I can ask or imagine. According to Your power, transform me so that I continually abide in You. Help me rebuild integrity with my family and my world. Revive me. Restore unto me the joy of Your salvation. According to Your power, be glorified in my life."

Action step: End every phone call or letter to your children with "I love you." Passionately foster loving relationships. God is love, and we are to live in love.

Questions for reflection/discussion:
1. How important is it to you to restore broken relationships with your children and family? What daily and weekly steps are you taking to accomplish this?
2. Name some reasonable, measureable, realistic, timely, and specific goals that you can work toward each day to help you establish meaningful communication with your family.
3. Why do you think the prophet Malachi refers to restoration of fathers and their children as being significant before the day of the Lord?

Chapter 15: Hope Is Not My Enemy

I wrote this book on drawing close to God through prayer after what I believe was only the first half of my life. I say the first half because I now believe it is only half time. Of course, only God knows and controls all things, and He may still call the game early under the mercy rule. He is God, and He does what He pleases (Ps. 115:3). At the end of the first half of my life, the odds of any kind of come back became so stacked against me and unrealistic that I had utterly given up. I had always believed that winners never quit and quitters never win. Even so, my faith in God became depleted under severe distress and disappointment as I experienced a powerful reverse in the failure of my business and life.

My second book, *Hope Is Not My Enemy*, is a memoir of the first half of my life and describes the details and some of the things I learned during that mysterious period when all of life left me in a hurry. I entered a seemingly endless tunnel of darkness that morphed into a hopeless downward spiral. It was the valley of the shadow of death and tears that I had feared all my life. For some reason, I never thought I would be forced to walk through such horror, and if I did, it would never last this long. As of today it has been six years. There have been times when I felt certain, 100 percent sure, that life was over. Traumatized, everything led to a destroyed life. I could see no future, and after so many simultaneous letdowns, hope truly became my enemy. I could not find God. He was hidden from my sight. I stopped putting my hope in Him.

I believed that I should condemn and avoid optimism as a means to avoid further disappointment and ridicule. Intentionally reserved and exhausted, all I wanted to do was pull into my protective position of death and away from additional catastrophes. Intolerable conflicts wore me down and made me cynical and apathetic—destroyed me.

Anxiety in the heart of man causes depression. (Prov. 12:25)

The losses I experienced were overwhelming. To have to report such disaster to my family, friends, and investors only left me sour and bitter. All sorts of self-condemnation took over, and my adversary and accuser, the devil, never let up. Sometimes he whispered, and other times he roared. My confidence in God and myself was gone. Emerson (1843) said, "If I have lost confidence in myself, I now have the whole universe against me."[1] No example of this could be truer than it was for me. My mistakes stabbed my soul over and over again as resentment and rage seethed into my usually optimistic and trusting nature. Publicly, I tried to stay calm and controlled, but inside I held back intense emotion. After exhausting every possibility to recover financial losses, I felt the crushing burden of piled-up disappointments so that I could not brave it any longer.

I had no choice but to accept my plight of losing everything I had worked so hard for and everything that mattered to me. My family, friends, and clients had put their trust in me, and I had let them down. However, it was not with malicious intent, greed, or the intended evil that prompts criminals to commit fraud for their own personal gain. Actually, the exact opposite was true. My sole purpose was to help recover losses, not hurt anyone—especially investors who I knew and had effectively served for many years. Everyone needed me not to fail them, but I did. I sobbed in sorrow and looked to the hills from where my help had always come, but this time, it seemed there was no help. My heart daily hardened in disappointment as I fought to hold back unshed tears.

Bitterness and Unbelief

For the first time in my life, I was forced to experience a reality that I had preached and counseled against since first learning of the forgiveness and grace of God: bitterness and unbelief. They became poison to my soul. I was bitter at God, myself, and soon the entire world. The thing about my life was that I intentionally avoided spending time with bitter, ego-centered, and mean people. Before then, I could not understand how anyone could be so resentful toward God and life. I liked to smile, laugh, joke, and have fun. Joy was natural for me. I never wanted to miss any adventure. My eyes were bright and opened wide to every dream of each day. Nevertheless, this new bitterness led quickly to an insidious sickness I had never known in even one day of my peaceful Christian life: morbid depression. I believed God had abandoned me. I felt like the prophet Elijah when he said, "Lord, I've had enough. Take my life."[2]

From April 2011 until March 2014, I experienced 1,052 sleepless and fitful nights. It was a different type of maelstrom. The psalmist says, "You have held my eyelids open; I am so troubled that I can not sleep."[3] I was oppressed and possessed by a spirit of death as my reasons for living were engulfed in a darkness that consumed me. Defeated and in diminished capacity, I left everything that mattered with no reason to believe that I would ever return.

When I departed on June 16, 2012, I did not think life could get any more ominous. This was bottom number one. Looking back, I now think of this entire period as stock chart pattern where a classic double bottom has been steadily put in place before a new ascent begins. During that time I wanted to die and simply be in God's eternal presence because in my body of sin, flesh, and disappointment, I felt separated from God. I knew how close I had felt and how much I loved God. I knew the joy of times past, but at that time, my faith became empty. I did not realize it, but my running was from Him. I felt like I had forgotten who God was and that He had forgotten me.

Tell Me about Yourself

My eyelids instantly filled with tears when I read a story that Marcus Borg shared in his book, *The Heart of Christianity, Rediscovering a Life of Faith*. A little girl found out that she was going to be a big sister! After her parents brought her newborn brother home from the hospital, the girl asked her parents for some private time alone with her newly delivered baby brother. She shut the door behind her. Her parents listened closely outside the door as their daughter leaned over the crib and whispered loudly, "Tell me about God," the little girl said to her confused baby brother, "I've almost forgotten."[4]

October 28, 2014, was another beat down, and the second bottom of the classic stock chart pattern that signals a turn around. On that day, I was sentenced to federal prison. I left the courtroom in chains, condemnation, and alienation as one forsaken with the absolute hell beat out of me. I had spent ten months in the county jail, and my physical strength was gone. I had lost twenty-one pounds from the poor conditions, stress, and malnourishment of that environment. Mercy and grace were nowhere to be found. Hope was gone, and I considered hope my enemy. I left saying to myself no more hoping for anything anymore. Three days later I was curled up in a defensive, fetal position on a concrete bench in a different yet freezing jail holding—cell in Florida. I was surrounded by angry, unknown, and indifferent faces. My life was broken into a million pieces. In those moments of silence, I began to silently pray the only thing I knew to pray, "God. Tell me about Yourself. I've almost forgotten."

Kierkegaard says that faith would not exist without doubt. Over the past six years, I have come to love the compassionate prayer in Jude 25, which says, "Be merciful to those who doubt." I had become more like the man who brought his demon-possessed son to Jesus who said to the troubled father, "All things are possible to him who believes." The man cried out with a Mickey Mouse answer, "I believe. Help my unbelief."[5] Jesus went on to heal the man's son even though the man sincerely expressed his doubts. That's me too. Often times I find myself bending God's ear with prayers like, "Please, please, please have mercy on me Lord Jesus, for I am a sinner and sometimes I doubt You. Help me trust You again."[6]

I wish I had always lived with the simple, constant, and obedient childlike faith that easily trusts God in all things. Yet, here is what I have found: my strongest beliefs are those I have had to wrestle with in the depths of my pain, prison, and darkness. Doubt and loss of hope forced me to desperately turn to my first and only love and to seek God more intensely, and every time, in the end, I find it deepens the richness of my faith and strengthens the hope and the love I long for.

My favorite quote that I have meditated on in prison is by German theologian Strifter. He wrote, "Pain is a holy angel who shows treasure to men which otherwise remains forever hidden. Through pain, men become greater than through all the joys of the world."[7] I tell my children all the time, God does more through the trials of suffering than He will ever do through many years of easy living and the pursuit of miracles and signs. They understand this now, and as hard as it has been, they also have something in them that will always make them stronger than most of their peers who have not experienced such adversity.

Second Chances

As I close out this book, I find myself thinking about life itself, its whole object, meaning, and purpose. I think about what I have made of life, what I am doing with it now, and what is the ultimate future that is steadily before me. Quite inevitably, I look backward, wandering how I have conducted and comported myself, and yes, I am well aware of the parts of my life that I have a deep sense of dissatisfaction with. I realize that I have not always done what I should have done or what I intended to do. I have broken every law except one: I have always loved God and always will. My heart is eternally His.

  Because of the nature of prison, I am painfully aware and reminded daily of my failures and inadequacy, but at the same time, I am aware of an even stronger and godly desire to do better than ever and accomplish more in the days that may lie ahead of me. I stress that all my ills and unhappiness of recent years ultimately come back to the fact that I wandered from the path of obedience to God. They are my mistakes, and I own them. I can improve myself here and there, but if I am centrally wrong with God or even a little wrong with God, even in small compromises, I am altogether wrong.

  In the latter years of his life and after many years of maturity, the apostle Peter humbly declared to the flock of God, "[F]or by His wounds you were healed. For you were continually straying like sheep, but now you have returned to the Shepherd and Guardian of your souls."[8] Peter knew a lot about failure and second chances. He, like the apostle Paul, made the most of the second chances he was given. Thankfully and amazingly, God is a God of many chances. He relentlessly pursues us with His compassion, which springs from His holiness, faithfulness, and grace.

Optimism

Today, I am drawn to optimism. It is the view that God inspires life and hope. It gives me strength to sustain each powerful reverse and claim that the best is yet to come. Optimism should never be despised! A righteous man falls seven times, but he always gets back up.[9] Failure is part of life, but optimism is will for the future. It has become my hope and vitality.

So, I remind you, "The Lord is near to the broken hearted and crushed in spirit."[10] God is closer to me—nearer to me than anything I have known or experienced. It is powerful and emotionally overwhelming. There is peace and contentment beyond anything I have ever known. Even in this dark, dungeon of a cell, which should not take much imagination for one to picture, the presence and love of God is more obvious than any other time in my life. I would not have known this great gain apart from this suffering.

Second-Half Recovery

Roy Riegels was an All-American center for the University of California Golden Bears football team. He played both offense and defense against Georgia Tech in the 1929 Rose Bowl. At the end of the first half, a Tech player on offense fumbled the ball. Roy picked up the loose ball and began running toward the goal line sixty-five yards away. The problem was that he was running toward the wrong goal line. One of Roy's teammates ran after him and tackled him just before he crossed the goal line for an opposing team touchdown.

Half time came, and Roy left the field in shame and embarrassment. He probably thought he would not get to play, nor finish the game that day and possibly not play football anymore. As the team sat in the locker room at half time, the only sound that Nibbs Price, the California coach, heard was Roy sitting in the corner crying like a baby. Finally coach stood and announced to the team, "Men, the same team that started the first half will start the second half."

Roy lifted his head. His eyes were red, and his face was wet with tears, "Coach, I can't do it. I've ruined you. I've ruined the University of California. I've ruined myself. I can't face that crowd in the stadium to save my life." Coach Price reached out his hand and said, "Roy. Get back up and go back in; the game is only half over!" It was said that Roy Riegels got up and gave one of the most inspiring efforts in Rose Bowl history.[11]

So now I say that we all know that we have run the wrong way. We have ruined our good names. We have stumbled and fallen, and we know the depths of our failures. But failure is not fatal. It is not the end. If you are afraid of failure, you will never try anything—especially anything interesting. You will take no risks.

This book is just one step on your path to fix things that are broken. Embrace your failures. Abandon the God "complex" that we have to be perfect in all things. Only God is perfect, so make your failures part of your story. View failure as engineering, trial and error, and learn to make mistakes in a good direction.

Henry Ford defined failure as the opportunity to start again more intelligently. I want to remind you of what my loyal pastor friend told me while I was in the dreadful county jail: "Lee. This is not the last chapter of your life. I know it, and you know it. The final chapter has not been written." The first part of my life did not end with a great success. I rose none. But now I realize that the game is not over. We have to get up, get back in the game, return to our first love of Christ, and let Him lead us to victory!

Hope Is Not My Enemy

In January of 2016, I walked the track at the Estill Federal Prison with a friend who had served nineteen years of his *draconian* twenty-eight-year sentence for drugs and a gun that started when he was twenty-five years old. He spent much of his time in prison learning the law and trying to help other prisoners find hope and freedom. On this particular day, he was somewhat downcast. While we were walking, I asked him if there was anything else he could do to get his time down and get out early. He seemed to have lost all hope and did not really want to talk about it. He said, "No. Every time a favorable law change would become close to passing to benefit me, it has gotten shot down by Congress." His next words made a huge impression on me. He said, "Hope is my enemy."

I walked in silence for the next lap and finally told him, "No. Hope is not your enemy. We can never lose hope. We are going to make it." I intensified my prayers for him.

Thirty days later he got a call from the public defender. He came to my cell to tell me the news that a motion would be filed on his behalf related to new law changes from the Johnson case. He kept his reserved composure as he talked about the possibility. In July of 2016, he was released from prison. After nineteen years of hell, he walked out the front gate with no chains and no cuffs. His parents picked him up, and he rode away a free man. I was sitting in solitary confinement when he left, but my heart rejoiced for him.

What made this even better is that my good friend Charlie Red who spent eighteen months by my side went home the very next week because of the same law changes. Both of them had eight years left on their sentences. Both of them had been on my daily prayer list. God miraculously answered our prayers. Keep praying. Keep trusting. Always keep hope. Hope is not our enemy!

We are in a waiting line to be released. One day, your name and my name will be called. Wait patiently. Wait for your love, and wait with your love.

I close with one of my favorite quotes:

> Do not be afraid to trust God utterly. As you go down the long corridor you may find that He has preceded you and locked many doors which you would fain have entered; but be sure that beyond these there is one which He has left unlocked. Open it and enter, and you will find yourself face to face with a bend of the river of opportunity, broader and deeper than anything you dared to imagine in your sunniest dreams. Launch forth on it; it conducts to the open sea. (F. B. Myer)[12]

Prayer: "So God, my Heavenly Father, rich in mercy and grace, lover of my soul. I love you too…with all my heart."

Questions for reflection/discussion:
1. Am I on an upward path?
2. What paths do I need to completely forget? Cross-reference: Isaiah 43:18.

Chapter 16: Chuck

Chuck Norris was his nickname. He and I shared a cell on and off for almost seventeen months. Chuck, like me, was the black sheep of his family—an ole good for nothing who had soiled his family reputation. Heroin had him in a choke hold, and according to him, his nerves were shrinking from anxiety. Each of his arms had three eight-inch scars from eighteen years of needle use. Chuck was weighed down by repeated failures, lost hope, and a sense of worthlessness. His only dream was to go home, move into a trailer his brother had prepared for him, and be with his two children and his brothers. He longed for one last chance at a new start. He was an intelligent, skilled car mechanic and at one time successfully ran his own repair shop and garage.

When I arrived at federal prison, I was glad to have Chuck as a friend. Even though we came from different backgrounds, his humble, plainspoken, and laid back disposition helped me to feel at ease. He spent most of his time in prison reading. He especially liked Hemmingway, and we discussed all kinds of genre. When I wrote this book on prayer, he poured over it at least three different times for me, and when I finished my memoir, *Hope Is Not My Enemy*, he read it at least five times, asking me pertinent questions and wanting me to retell life stories for him in real time.
In prison, Chuck spent many of his days trying to find a fix, assemble some type of rig, and experience the temporary escape of a short-term high. He constantly sought a cigarette and did odd jobs like carrying people's laundry and washing stamps to pay his bills. While he still had a couple of years to the door, and he could not wait to go home, he was also fearful of the temptation of what he would face once he walked out the front gate with no chains or shackles. He commented many times that a good bag of dope and a street whore would probably kill him.

After about two months of us sharing a cell together, Chuck committed his life to Christ. While it was a beautiful thing to watch him revel in the beauty of the gospel, it was also a difficult task for both of us. Living in the same small cell means you know almost everything about the other person. Salvation is step one, but sanctification (changing into the image of Christ) is a lifelong battle of suffering, struggles, and the occasional pleasant surprise. In his mind and spirit, he tried a number of times to give up various poisons and nicotine, but his body would not let him. His thinking was impaired, and his body chemically dependent. I found trying to keep him off any kind of drug impossible. On several occasions, I watched him fight withdrawals to the point of sweating and chills.

Finding and building his relationship with Christ gave him a new peace. He smiled at me when he finished reading the entire New Testament for the first time in one month. He then read it several more times along with the book of Psalms and Proverbs. He was learning how to contemplatively pray each day. He also loved the story by Hemmingway about a Spanish father who decided to reconcile with his son who had run away to Madrid. Remorseful for how he treated his son, the father took out an advertisement in the national newspaper *El Liberal* that said, "PACO MEET ME AT HOTEL MONTANA NOON TUESDAY. ALL IS FORGIVEN. PAPA." Paco is a common name in Spain, and when the father traveled to the square to find his lost son, he found eight hundred young men named Paco waiting for their fathers.

Philip Yancey writes, "Hemingway knew about the ungrace of families. His devout parents—Hemingway's grandparents had attended evangelical Wheaton College—detested Hemingway's libertine life, and after a time his mother refused to allow him in her presence. One year for his birthday, she mailed him a cake along with the gun his father had used to kill himself. Another year she wrote him a letter explaining that a mother's life is like a bank. 'Every child that is born to her enters the world with a large and prosperous bank account, seemingly inexhaustible. The child,' she continued, 'makes withdrawals but no deposits during all the early years. Later, when the child grows up, it is his responsibility to replenish the supply he has drawn down.' Hemingway's mother then proceeded to spell out all the specific ways in which Ernest should be making deposits to keep the account in good standing: flowers, fruit or candy, a surreptitious paying of Mother's bills, and above all a determination to stop 'neglecting your duties to God and your Savior, Jesus Christ.' Hemingway never got over his hatred for his mother or for her Savior."

Chuck had long, sandy-brown mullet-styled hair, big blue eyes, and only a couple of teeth. I joked with him about brushing his two teeth and that he should consider turning the water on and using some soap when he got into the shower. He had been arrested forty-nine different times in his life. Every morning he quietly woke up and said, "I hate this miserable place."

I would say, "I can't tell."

There were many times that my gloomy friend depression would beat me with a bat, and it was my friend Buck who knew how to help me. His humor, stories, and never-ending desire to keep me encouraged pushed me through the darkness. He would often say, "Price. Life is a gamble, but we are still in the game. It's not over yet."

I remember one evening after I had visited with my family in visitation that I was so down I could barely hold my head up. There is nothing worse than watching your loved one walk out the front gate in freedom while you have to go back to prison alone. So that night I skipped chow and went to the yard. I walked in solitude for two and half hours while wiping away tear after tear without anyone seeing me. When I came back to my cell, I smiled because Chuck had fixed two homemade pepperoni's pizzas with two Mountain Dews on ice. He turned on some "rigged up" speakers to his radio, and we listened to country music for a couple of hours. He told me stories of all the crazy women, drugs, fights, and people he had met, his pet goat riding in his boat on the river, his pet duck getting hit by an eighteen-wheeler, and the embarrassment he underwent when he messed his pants on a job site because he didn't get to the port-a-potty in time. He shared details of the many times he spent with his various woman friends while shooting heroine at the Covered Wagon Hotel, and the time he almost blew up himself and his mistress lighting the gas heater in the room. He laughed when he would say, "For twenty dollars a night, the woman at the hotel front desk asked no questions."

Every story was full of spice and self-depreciating humor, but then he would always circle around to his struggle with God's forgiveness. He wished he could get better and advance in his spiritual life. Like all of us, he had a hard time detaching from past struggles while saying "yes" to God in everything. Nonetheless, I believe it was his sincere desire to establish deeper communion with the Lord, and I was glad God placed him in my life.

Each night he made sure to remind me to lead us in prayer. If I was too sleepy, he would wake me up just to remind me to pray. He would always say "thank you" after the prayer, and then, he would go right to sleep. In late April of 2016, he became very sick, and he could not breathe. Some nights I would stay up with him helping him sit up and breathe, and for hours we would pray. I would quote passages of scripture like Psalm 23 or 1 Corinthians 13 and then keep on praying for him. He needed to be transferred to a medical facility, but the prisoner is at the mercy of a bureaucratic system that requires paperwork be touched by ten different people until someone finally says, "No." Chuck hated going out to the hospital. They placed him in cuffs, chains, and a black box. His arms would bruise and scratch easily from the cuffs and the black box.

One of our last conversations was that he wanted to make sure his brothers knew to put him in a grave next to where his brothers would be buried. He did not want to be "buried off" somewhere by himself and all alone. Like all of us, he had a deep fear of abandonment. More than anything, he worried about what happened in the next life and making it to heaven. I asked Chuck, "Do you have faith?"

He said, "Yes. I believe in Jesus for my salvation. I have asked him to forgive me my sins, and received Him into my heart."

I said, "Then you have victory. Faith is the victory that overcomes the world (1 John 5:3). To be absent from the body is to be present with the Lord. For you to live is Christ, but when death comes, you will have great gain (Phil. 1:21).

The day you die is the day you will be in paradise with the Lord just like the thief on the cross (Luke 23:43)." I continued, "Chuck, you need to know one thing about God. He is not mad at you. He is a lovesick Father who never stops thinking about you. His grace is more than sufficient for all your past sins. There is nothing you can do to separate yourself from His love and peace. There is no condemnation for those who are in Christ Jesus—past, present, and future—your sins are paid for. He forgives you. He receives. He adopts. He embraces you. He is yours. You are His. You are bought with a price. His hand is stretched out for you (Isa. 10:4). Do not worry or fear. Trust Him. For God so loved "Chuck Norris" that He gave Himself for you that if you believe in His Son, Jesus Christ, you will not perish but have eternal life."

Chuck said, "Price, I have not made it to advanced contemplation as you talk about, but I believe Jesus is my Savior."

In late May 2016, Chuck was cuffed, chained, and taken out of prison to a hospital. When prisoners are taken out to a hospital, they are never told where they are going. He could hardly breathe and was in bad shape. He suffered alone in an unknown hospital bed for five days with one arm cuffed to the top rail and one ankle cuffed to the bottom rail of the bed. Two guards were always near by. His family was not notified until the day he died that he was even in the hospital. They were unable to travel to South Carolina hospital near Estill in time to see him. He died at age fifty-one, alone, not having an opportunity to hug or hold a hand and say goodbye to his children and brothers.

At first I was disappointed because I wanted to see him free and go home. I wanted to hear about how he hugged his children and made peace with his past adversaries. I wanted to hear about him finding a church community, overcoming addictions, starting a new life, and getting the health care he needed to extend his life. But then I realized that God left Chuck here for me and used Chuck to give me a much-needed friend, inspire me and help me overcome my loneliness. And Chuck? He made it to freedom and a permanent home in heaven with Jesus where there is no more sin, sickness, suffering, and tears.

God's Everlasting Love

When I think about the stories in the various gospels given to us by Jesus, there is a clear picture formed in my mind of the desperation and recklessness of our God searching, looking, waiting, and pleading for us to come to Him. Jesus said, "Come to Me all of you who are weary" (Matt. 11:28). To illustrate the Father's great love for humanity, Jesus tells the story of the woman who desperately searches all night until she finds her lost and very valuable coin. She is ecstatic! Then He tells us about the shepherd who leaves the ninety-nine sheep to hunt in the darkness for that one lost sheep that has gone astray. When the sheep is found, the shepherd is happy. And then Jesus tells of the father of the lost son who left home with his inheritance and squandered it away on whiskey, women, and gambling. But his father searches over the fields day and night hoping, pleading, and begging for his lost son to return home. When he sees his prodigal in the far distance, the father runs to meet him and throws a jubilant party because he is reunited with his son. (Luke 15).

We all dream of the day when we will walk out of the front gates of prison with no chains to the ones we love, and what a celebration it will be! But it is nothing compared to the joyful eruption of all the angels in the celestial glory of God's heaven, trillions of light-years away from here in an unimaginable splendor, where Chuck is now, who rejoice at just one who repents and comes home to the Father. This is love! Not that we loved Him, but that He loved us first and sent His Son as an atoning sacrifice for our sins (1 John 4:10)!

Bibliography

Archer, Gleason. *Encyclopedia of Bible Difficulties.* Grand Rapids, MI: Zondervan, 1982.

Bonhoeffer, Dietrich. *The Cost of Discipleship.* New York: MacMillan, 1959.

Borg, Marcus. *The Heart of Christianity, Rediscovering A Life of Faith.* San Francisco, CA: Harper One, 2003.

Bounds, E. M. *The Complete Works of EM Bounds.* Grand Rapids, MI: Baker Books, 1990.

Buechner, Frederick. *The Magnificent Defeat.* New York: Seabury, 1979.

Calvin, John. *Institutes of the Christian Religion.* Grand Rapids, MI: Erdmans, 1964.

Carmichael, Amy. *Edge of His Ways.* Fort Washington, PA: Christian Literature Crusader, 1995.

Dubay, Thomas. *Fire Within.* San Francisco, CA: Ignatuius Press, 1989.

Dunn, Ron. *Don't Just Stand There, Pray Something.* Nashville, TN: Thomas Nelson, 1992.

Elliott, Elizabeth. *A Chance to Die, the life and Legacy of Amy Charmichael.* Ada, MI: Revell, 1987.

Finney, Charles. *Prevailing Prayer.* Grand Rapids, MI: Kregel, 1965.

Gordon, S. D. *Quiet Talks on Prayer.* Old Tapper, NJ: Fleming H. Powell, 1967.

Jones, Martin-Lloyd. *Preaching and Preachers.* Grand Rapids, MI: Eerdmans, 1972.

Kant, Immanuel. Quoted in Frederich Heiler, *Prayer*, p. 89. New York: Oxford University Press, 1932.

Kierkegaard, Soren. *Philosophical Fragments.* Translated by David Swenson. Princeton, NJ: Princeton University Press, 1962.

Lawrence, Brother, *Practice of the Presence of God with Spiritual Maxims.* Grand Rapids, MI: Spire Books, 2000.

Lewis, C. S. *Mere Christianity.* New York: MacMillan, 1960.

Lord, Peter. *Hearing God.* Grand Rapids, MI: Baker Books, 1988.

Lutzer, Erwin W. *7 Reasons Why You Can Trust the Bible.* Chicago, IL: Moody Press, 1998.

MacArthur, John. *Slave.* Nashville, TN: Thomas Nelson, 2010.

Meyer, F. B. *Elijah and the Secret of His Power.* www.Bibleteacher.org, 2006.

Murray, Andrew. *Abiding in Christ.*

Nouwen, Henri J. M. *The Wounded Healer.* New York: Random House, 1972.

Orr, J. Edwin Orr. *The Eager Feet.* Chicago, IL: Moody Press, 1975.

Paschal, Blaise. *Pensees.* New York: Dutton, 1958.

Peck, Scott M. *The Road Less Traveled.* New York: Touchstone, 1978.

Progoff, Ira. *The Cloud of Unknowing.* Translated by Ira Progoff. Julian Press, 1957.

Smedes, Lewis B. *How Can It Be All Right When Everything Is All Wrong?* San Francisco, CA: Harper & Row, 1959.

Sproul, R. C. *The Consequences of Ideas.* Wheaton, IL: Crossway, 2000.

Spurgeon, C. H. *Exposition of Psalm 42.* Metropolitan Tabernacle Pulpit, vol. 60.

Stanley, Charles F. *How to Listen to God.* Nashville, TN: Thomas Nelson, 1985.

———. *10 Principles for Studying Your Bible.* Nashville, TN: Thomas Nelson, 2008.

Strobel, Lee. *The Case for Christ.* Grand Rapids, MI: Zondervan, 1998.

St. Teresa. *Way of Perfection.*

Swindall, Chuck. *The Apostle Paul.*

Teresa, Mother. *Everything Starts from Prayer.* Ashland, OR: White Cloud Press, 1998.

Thielicke, Helment. *The Waiting Father.* San Francisco, CA: Harper & Row, 1987.

Tozer, A. W. *Echoes form Eden.* Harrisburg, PA: Christian Publications, 1981.

———. *The Pursuit of God.* Mockingbird Classic Publishing, 2016.

Wink, Walter. *Naming the Powers: The Language of Power in the New Testament.* Philadelphia, PA: Fortress Press, 1984.

Yancey, Philip. *Disappointment with God.* Grand Rapids, MI: Zondervan, 1988.

———. *The Jesus I Never Knew.* Grand Rapids, MI: Zondervan, 1995.

Appendix 1
Thirty Must-Read Books for the Growing Christian

1. *Pursuit of Holiness* by Jerry Bridges
2. *The Holiness of God* by R. C. Sproul
3. *The Jesus I Never Knew* by Philip Yancey (my personal favorite)
4. *Purpose Driven Life* by Rick Warren
5. *Trusting God* by Jerry Bridges
6. *The Consequences of Ideas* by R. C. Sproul
7. *Celebration of Discipline* by Richard Foster
8. *The Road Less Traveled* by Scott Peck
9. *Overcoming Temptation* by Dr. Charles Stanley
10. *Forgiveness* by Dr. Charles Stanley
11. *7 Reasons Why You Can Trust the Bible* by Erwin W. Lutzer
12. *The Case for Christ* by Lee Strobel
13. *Anchor for the Soul* by Ray Pritchard
14. *Practicing the Presence of God* by Brother Lawrence
15. *Every Man's Battle* by Stephen Arterburn
16. *Mere Christianity* by C. S. Lewis
17. *Desiring God* by John Piper
18. *Cost of Discipleship* by Dietrich Bonhoeffer
19. *Future Grace* by John Piper
20. *Beyond All You Could Ask or Think* by Ray Pritchard
21. *Master Plan of Evangelism* by Robert Coleman
22. *Hearing God* by Peter Lord
23. *Foxe's Book of Martyrs* by John Foxe
24. *Disciple Making Pastor* by Bill Hull
25. *What's Amazing about Grace* by Philip Yancey
26. *The Insanity of God* by Nik Pipkin
27. *Knowing God* by J.I. Packer
28. *Radical* by David Platt
29. *Ragamuffin Gospel* by Brenning Manning
30. *The Pleasures of God* by John Piper

Appendix II
History of the English Bible

1. The Bible is made up of sixtysix different books that were written over sixteen hundred years from approximately 1500 BC to AD 95. There were forty different inspired authors who were prophets, leaders, kings, priests, and eyewitness followers of Jesus. The Old Testament has thirty nine books, written between 1500 and 400 BC. The New Testament has twenty seven books written between AD 45 to AD 95.
2. The Old Testament was originally written in Hebrew, with some Aramaic. The New Testament was originally written in Greek.
3. The books of the Bible were collected, arranged, and recognized as inspired sacred authority by councils of rabbis and councils of church leaders based on careful guidelines.
4. Before the printing press was invented in AD 1450, the Bible was copied by hand. The Bible was copied very accurately and carefully, by special scribes who developed intricate methods of counting words and letters to ensure that no errors had been made.
5. The Bible was the first book ever printed on the printing press with moveable type (Gutenberg Press, 1455, Latin Bible).
6. There is much evidence that the Bible we have today is remarkably true to the original writings. Of the thousands of copies made by hand before AD 1500, nearly 5,900 Greek manuscripts from the New Testament alone still exist today. The text of the Bible is better perservered than the writings of Plato or Aristotle.
7. The discovery of the Dead Sea Scrolls in 1948 confirmed the astonishing reliability of some of the copies of the Old Testament made over the years. Although some spelling variations exist, no variation affects the message or basic doctrines of the Bible.
8. As the Bible was carried to other countries, it was translated into the common language of the people by scholars who wanted others to know God's Word. Today there

are still over two thousand people groups with no Bible in their own language.

9. By AD 200, the Bible was translated into seven languages; by AD 500, the Bible was translated into thirteen languages. By AD 900, seventeen languages; by 1400, twenty eight languages, by 1800, fifty seven languages; by 1900, five hundred thirty seven languages; by 1980, eleven hundred languages; by 2006, two thousand four hundred twenty six languages have some portion of the Bible translated into their language.

10. Portions of the Old Testament were written on stone tablets (Exodus 20). Others were written on clay and others on leather. Scrolls of leather, and later papyrus, were used to make copies of the Scriptures. During the New Testament times, papyrus was used. The oldest New Testament fragment (from John 18) that we have today was copied on a papyrus codex around AD 110-130.

11. Papyrus, a plant, is cut into strips and pressed into sheets of writing material and can be made into a scroll or a codex. The New Testament books were probably first written on papyrus scrolls. Later, Christians began to copy them on sheets of papyrus which are bound and placed between two pieces of wood for covers. This form of early book is known as codex.

12. Jesus quoted the Old Testament scriptures often. He says that He did not come to destroy the Scriptures, but to fulfill them. He said to his disciples, "These are My words which I spoke to you while I was still with you, that all things which are written about Me in the Law of Moses and the Prophets and the Psalms must be fulfilled. Then He opened their minds to understand the Scriptures, and He said unto them, 'Thus, it is written, that the Christ would suffer and rise again from the dead on the third day." (Luke 24:27, 46)

13. Matthew, Mark, Luke, John, Paul, James, Peter and Jude wrote the Gospels, history, letters to other Christians, and the Revelation between AD 45-95. The writers quote from all but eight Old Testament books. These writings in Greek were copied and circulated so that by about AD 150, there was wide

enough use of them to speak of the "New Testament" or "New Covenant." The New Covenant that God made with His people was promised in Jeremiah 31:31-34 and referred to by Jesus in Luke 22:20. Paul referred to it in 1 Corinthians 11:25. The letter to the Hebrews also addressed the new covenant comprehensively.

14. Evidence delivered from the first century AD Jewish writers Philo and Josephus indicates that the Old Testament Hebrew Canon did not include the Apocrypha.

15. Church fathers accepted the writings of the Gospels and Paul's letters as canonical (from a Greek word referring to the rule of faith and truth). Origen lists twenty one approved New Testament books. Eusebius lists twenty two accepted books.

16. The New Testament books are collected and circulated throughout the Mediterranean about the time of Constantine, the Roman Emperor who legalized Christianity in AD 313. By AD 400, the standard twenty seven New Testament books is accepted in the East and West as confirmed by Athanasius, Jerome, Augustine, and three church councils. The twenty seven books of the New Testament were formally confirmed as canonical by the Synod of Carthage in AD 397, thus recognizing three centuries of use by the followers of Christ.

17. Jerome starts translating the Scriptures into Latin in AD 382 and finishes twenty three years later. This translation, called the Latin Vulgate, remains the basic Bible for many centuries.

18. Over time, fine animal skins from calves and antelope (vellum), and sheep's and goats (parchment) were used over the next one thousand years to make copies of the Bible from approximately AD 300-1400s.

19. Wycliffe Bibles were inscribed by hand on vellum in the 1300s-1400s. Some copies took ten months to two years to produce and the cost was over a year's wages. The Bible was the first book to be printed with the Gutenberg printing press in 1455.

20. The bible began with God telling Moses to write in a book. Kings, leaders and prophets of Israel all did the same thing as God led them. One thousand years later, Ezra, a priest and

scribe (a meticulous or careful writer), collected and arranged the Hebrew Bible or Old Testament around 450 BC.

21. The Septuagint is the Greek Translation of the Hebrew Bible or Old Testament. The Old Testament was translated into Greek around 250 BC by Jewish Scholars and Scribes in Alexandria, Egypt (Where Alexander the Great was embalmed-the city is now underwater). The word Septuagint means seventy referring to the tradition that 70 or 72 men translated it. It is often abbreviated LXX, the Latin Roman Numeral for seventy. The Septuagint includes the Apocrypha (meaning "hidden"), referring to the seven books that were originally included in the Hebrew Bible until AD 90 when they were removed by Jewish leaders.

22. From AD 378-600 the Roman empire declined. Germanic migrations caused new languages to emerge.

23. The Masoretics are special Jewish Scribes entrusted with the sacred task of making copies of the Hebrew Scriptures (Old Testament) approximately during AD 500-900. They developed a meticulous system of counting the number of words in each book of the Bible to make sure they had copied it correctly. Any scroll found to have an error was buried or burned according to Jewish law.

24. Christianity reached Britain before AD 300, but Anglo-Saxon pagans drove Christian Briton into Wales (AD 450-600). In AD 596, Augustine of Canterbury began evangelization again.

25. Caedmon, an illiterate monk, retells portions of Scripture in Anglo-Saxon (Old English) poetry (AD 676).

26. Aldhelm of Sherburne, AD 709, is said to have translated the Psalms into Anglo-Saxon.

27. Bede, a monk and scholar, makes an Old English (Anglo-Saxon) translation of portions of Scripture. On his deathbed in AD 735, he finishes translating the Book of John.

28. Alfred the Great, King of Wessex (AD 871-901) translates portions of Exodus, Psalms, and Acts.

29. Alfred, Bishop of Durham, inserts a translation in the Northumbrian dialect between the lines of the Lindisfarne Gospels around AD 950.

30. Aelfric (AD 955-1020) translated portions of the Old Testament.
31. Normans conquer England (AD 1066) and make French the official language. No English translation work is produced again until the 1300s.
32. Old Anglo Saxon English develops and Middle English emerges, popularized by works such as the Canterbury Tales and Richard Rolle's Psalter (1340).
33. Finally, the first English Bible is translated from Latin in 1382, and is called the Wycliffe Bible in honor of priest and Oxford scholar, John Wycliffe. During his lifetime, Wycliffe had wanted common people to have the Bible. He also criticized a number of church practices and policies. His followers, derisively call Lollards (meaning "mumblers"), including criticisms in the preface to the Wycliffe Bible. The Bible is banned and burned. Forty years after Wycliffe's death, his bones are exhumed and burned for heresy.
34. In 1408, in England, it becomes illegal to translate or read the Bible in common English without permission of the Bishop.
35. The world's first printing press with moveable metal type is invented in 1455 in Germany by Johann Gutenberg. This invention is perhaps the single most important event to influence the spread of the Bible.
36. The Gutenberg Bible is the first book ever printed. This Latin Vulgate version is often illuminated by artist who hand painted letters and ornaments on each page.
37. Erasmus, a priest and Greek scholar, published a new Greek edition and a more accurate Latin translation of the New Testament in 1516. His goal was that everyone be able to read the Bible, from the farmer in the field to the weaver at the loom. Erasmus' Greek text forms the basis of the "Textus Receptus" and was used by later by Martin Luther, William Tyndale and the King James translators.
38. William Tyndale, a priest and Oxford scholar, translates the New Testament from Greek in 1525, but cannot get approval to publish it in England. He moves to Germany and prints Bibles, smuggling them into England in sacks of corn and flour. In 1533 he publishes part of the Old Testament

translated from Hebrew. in 1536, Tyndale was strangled and burned at the stake. His final words are, "Lord, open the King of England's eyes." Tyndale is called the "Father of the English Bible," because his translation forms the basis of the King James Version. Much of the style and vocabulary we know as "Biblical English" is traceable to his work.

39. Other Bibles were translated like the Coverdale Bible (AD 1535), and was dedicated to Anne Boleyn, King Henry VIII's wife. This is the first complete Bible to be printed in English.

40. Matthew's Bible, translated by John Rogers under the pen name, "Thomas Matthew," was first published with the King's permission (AD 1537). Printed just one year after Tyndale's death, its New Testament relies heavily on Tyndale's version, and even has a tribute to him on the last page of the Old Testament. Later, Thomas Cromwell, advisor to King Henry VIII, entrusts Coverdale to revise Matthew's Bible to make a Great Bible. The Great Bible (AD 1539) is placed in every church by order of Thomas Cranmer, archbishop under King Henry VIII. The Bible is chained to the church pillars to discourage theft.

41. In AD 1555, England's Queen Mary bans protestant translations of the English Bible. John Rogers and Thomas Cranner are burned at the stake. Later, some 300 men, women and children are also burned. The nickname, "Bloody Mary," is given to her rule.

42. Exiles from England flee to Geneva, Switzerland, and in 1560, they print the Geneva Bible, a complete revision of the Great Bible with Old Testament translated from Hebrew. The Geneva Bible contains theological notes from Protestant scholars John Calvin, Beza, Knox, and Whittingham. It is the first Bible to use Roman type instead of black letter. This is the Bible of Shakespeare and the one carried to America by the Pilgrims in 1620. The 1640 edition is the first English Bible to omit the Apocrypha.

43. A new translation begins under Queen Elizabeth in 1568. It is translated by several bishops of the Church of England in answer to the Geneva Bible.

44. The Rheims-Douai Bible was translated into English from

the Latin Vulgate by Catholic Scholar Gregory Martin, while in exile in France. He completed the New Testament in 1582 and the Old Testament in 1609. It becomes the standard translation for the Catholic Church.

45. King James I of England commissions 54 scholars to undertake a new Bible translation. Over the next six years, six teams of scholars using the Bishops Bible and Tyndale's Bible, as well as available Greek and Hebrew manuscripts, complete the new version in 1611. The King James Version (called the "Authorized Version," even though King James never gave the finished version his royal approval) is revised several times. The edition used today was revised in 1769.

46. There are now hundreds of modern translations including the English Revised Version (1885), the American Standard Version (1901), which is the revision of the King James Version into American English. There is also the Moffat Bible (1926), and many others. The 1971 New American Standard is a literal, word for word translation. The New International Version (NIV) is a phrase for phrase translation.

47. Between 1629 and 1947, several of the earliest known copies of the Bible are found. Codex Alexandrinus, a copy of the New Testament from about AD 400, was made available to Western Scholars.

48. Codex Sinaiticus, the earliest complete copy of the New Testament, copied in AD 350, was found in St. Catherine's Monastery near Mt. Sinai, Arabia.

49. Each revision is designed to reflect changes to the current language and findings from manuscripts discovered from the two previous centuries. The goal is to use better Hebrew and Greek texts and to retranslate words based on new linguistic information about ancient Hebrew.

50. Codex Vaticanus, the earliest and best known copy of the New Testament from AD 350 was released in 1889 by the Vatican Library.

51. In 1947, the Dead Sea Scrolls, found in a cave by a shepherd, contain the oldest known copies of portions of the Old Testament. These copies were made between 100 BC and AD 100. A scroll of Isaiah that is part of the Dead Sea

Scrolls is the oldest complete manuscript of any book of the Bible. The copies of the Isaiah manuscript discovered in the Qumran caves prove to be remarkably close to the standard Hebrew Bible, varying slightly in the spelling of some names. They give overwhelming confirmation of the reliability of the Masoretic copies. During the 1900s more than 100 New Testament manuscripts are found in Egypt.
.
Sources: The World Christian Encyclopedia, Wycliffe International, Gleason Archer, Bible Difficulties, Edwin Lutzer, Seven Reasons Why You Can Trust The Bible

Thank you for purchasing and reading this book. It was written as a gift to God and to help discouraged and hopeless prisoners and their families. All proceeds are used to purchase and send more books to prisoners. My parents have made a generous investment into this ministry, and helped me send this book to many prisoners.

I sincerely hope that this book encourages you to seek and trust God, and to further understand the significance of the revelation of His grace and overwhelming mercy. If you enjoyed this book a few kind words on the bookseller's review pages (Amazon and others) would be much appreciated. Good reviews are extremely beneficial to an author's career. Thank you from the depths of my heart if you will do that for me. I wish you the very best in your pursuit of God's truth and purpose for your life.

Please direct all comments and questions to:

Twil Publishing, LLC
PO Box 10144
Bradenton, Fl. 34282

Notes

Chapter 1

1. Gen. 29:20.
2. Ps. 46:10.
3. Charles H. Spurgeon, *All of Grace*, A Spurgeon Collection, 1st ed. (Lucid Books, 2013).

4. William Cowper and Humphrey Summer Milford, *The Poetical Works of William Cowper* (London: Oxford University Press, 1934).
5. Jer. 29:11.
6. Spurgeon, *All of Grace*.
7. Ps. 68:6.
8. Walter Wink, *The Powers That Be: Theology for a New Millennium* (New York: Doubleday, 1999), 185–86.
9. Gordon, *Quiet Talks on Prayer*.
10. Isa. 8:17.
11. Gen. 32:26.
12. Bounds, *Complete Works of EM Bounds*.
13. *Phillipians 1:12-13*

Chapter 2

1. Marie Durant, http://www.protestants.org/faq/histoire/htm/durant.htm.
2. Heb. 11:6.
3. Rom. 4:20.
4. Ps. 90:12.
5. Bonhoeffer, *Cost of Discipleship*.
6. Abraham Lincoln.
7. D. L. Moody, *The Life of Dwight L. Moody, Jr.*, 1st ed. (Charlotte, NC: Laymond, 2001).
8. Lawrence Cunningham, *Brother Francis*, 1st ed. (New York: Harper & Row, 1972).
9. Mother Teresa, *Everything Starts from Prayer*.
10. James 5:16.
11. Moody, *Life of Dwight L. Moody, Jr.*
12. Isa. 40:31.
13. Dubay, *Fire Within*.

Chapter 3

1. Matt. 5:27–28.
2. R. G. Lee, *Payday Someday*. It comes from a famous sermon preached by R. G. Lee. He preached this sermon more than one thousand times. The sermon is available online at www.newsforChristians.com.
3. Kierkegaard, *Philosophical Fragments*.
4. Ps. 131:3.
5. Luke 11:24–26.
6. Bonhoeffer, *Cost of Discipleship*.
7. Rom. 5:1.
8. Progoff, *The Cloud of Unknowing*.

Chapter 4

1. Rom. 12:2.
2. Ps. 63:1.
3. Ps. 42:1–2.
4. Matt. 6:33.
5. Ps. 110:1.
6. Matt. 5:23–24.
7. Heb. 4:16.
8. Lawrence, *Practice of the Presence of God*.

Chapter 5

1. Mark 8:34–38, 1:17.
2. Rom. 10:9–10.
3. Rom. 3:10, 3:23.
4. Ps. 19:12.
5. 2 Cor. 5:17.

6. Bob Pierce.
7. Kierkegaard, *Philosophical Fragments*.

Chapter 6
1. Matt. 9:36–37.
2. Heb. 4:15.
3. Oswald Chambers, *My Utmost for His Highest* (Grand Rapids, MI: Discovery House, 2006).

Chapter 7
1. Simon Armitage, *Homer's Odyssey* (London: Faber & Faber, 2007).
2. *Luke 6:27-28*
3. Rom. 5:10.
4. Matt. 5:23–24.
5. Matt. 18:34, 6:14–15.
6. Luke 7:37–51.
7. St. Francis of Assisi.

Chapter 8
1. Booker T. Washington.
2. Matt. 26:52.
3. *Legend of Moses*.
4. Luke 7:37–50.
5. Matt. 18:21.
6. Matt. 6:12–16.
7. Matt. 18:21–34.
8. Matt. 18:35.
9. 1 Cor. 13.
10. http://www.asiannews.it/index.php?/=conduit=90542theme.
11. Luke 23:34.

Chapter 9
1. James 1:15.
2. 1 Pet. 1:16; Heb. 12:14.
3. Matt. 18:6.
4. 1 John 5:16–17.
5. Peck, Scott. The Road Less Traveled. p. 24.
6. Ps. 52:1.
7. Rom. 1:26–32
8. 1 Thess. 4:3–4.
9. 2 Tim. 2:22.
10. Steve Chapman, "The Chase," chap. 7 in *A Look at Life from the Deer Stand* (Eugene, OR: Harvest House, 2009).
11. Gal. 6:7.
12. Stephen Arterburn, *Every Man's Battle* (Colorado Springs, CO: WaterBrook, 2009).
13. Phil. 4:13
14. Rom. 8:31.
15. *Encyclopedia Britannica Online*, s.v. "hubris."
16. Lewis, *Mere Christianity*
17. Yancey, *The Jesus I Never Knew*, 119.

Chapter 10
1. Mark 1:41.
2. John 1:1.
3. Luke 1:21–22.
4. Gen. 19:26.

5. Jonathon Edwards.
6. Luke 11:1.
7. Matt. 7:7.
8. Calvin, *Institutes of the Christian Religion*.
9. Lam. 3:25.
10. Lawrence, *Practice of the Presence of God*.
11. Origen, *An Exhortation to Martyrdom, Prayer, and Selected Works*, Classics of Western Spirituality, trans. Rowan Greer (New York: Paulist, 1972), 92.
12. Kant, *Prayer*, 89.
13. Jer. 33:3.
14. James 4:2–3.
15. George Muller, 1805–98.
16. James 5:16.
17. Charles Blondin.

Chapter 11
1. George Truett, former pastor of FBC of Dallas (1867–1944).
2. Hyatt, John, and Isaiah.
3. Phil. 2:4.
4. John 15:17.
5. 2 Cor. 10:3–5.
6. Benedict Spinoza, Dutch philosopher (1632–77).
7. Ralph Waldo Emerson.
8. Henry David Thoreau, Western philosopher (1817–62).

Chapter 12
1. Matt. 15:37–45.
2. Philip Zimbardo, *Psychology Today*.
3. Matt. 9:19–22.
4. Lev. 15:25–27.
5. G. Campbell Morgan, 1863–1945.
6. Isa. 55:6–8.
7. Yancey, *Disappointment with God*.
8. Ps. 34:18.
9. Thomas Aquinas, 1225–74.
10. C. S. Lewis, *A Grief Observed* (New York: Seabury, 1961).
11. Isa. 54:7, 43:1.
12. Bonhoeffer, *Cost of Discipleship*.
13. Annie Dillard.

Chapter 13
1. Frederick Douglas, 1818–95.
2. Ps. 119:67.
3. Otto Dibelius, German bishop (1880–1967).
4. Phil. 4:13.
5. Rom. 8:31.
6. Hudson Taylor.
7. Tozer, *Echoes form Eden*.
8. Phil. 1:6.
9. Rom. 8:28.
10. Sproul, *The Consequences of Ideas*.
11. Ps. 22:1.
12. C. I. Scoffield.
13. Martin Luther King.
14. Ralph Waldo Emerson.
15. Paschal, *Pensees*.
16. Albert Einstein.

17. Henry David Thoreau.
18. James 1:2–3.

Chapter 14

1. James 1:2–3.
2. Mother Teresa, *Everything Starts from Prayer*.
3. Peck, *The Road Less Traveled*, 25.
4. Buechner, *The Magnificent Defeat*, 65.
5. Eph. 5:18.
6. Mal. 4:5–6.
7. Carl Sandburg.
8. Rom. 8:28–29.
9. St. Augustine of Hippo 354–430.

Chapter 15

1. Ralph Waldo Emerson, 1803–82.
2. 1 Kings 19:4.
3. Ps. 77:4.
4. Borg, *The Heart of Christianity*, 114.
5. Mark 9:23–24.
6. Luke 18:13.
7. Strifter (quote from *Cost of Discipleship* by Dietrich Bonhoeffer).
8. 1 Pet. 2:24–25.
9. Prov. 24:16.
10. Ps. 34:18.
11. Roy Riegels, 1908–93.
12. F. B. Myers.

Made in United States
North Haven, CT
12 February 2022

15928591R00083